Le

Michael Buckley was born in Cork, Ireland, in 1924. He was educated at the Presentation College, Cork and the Gregorian University in Rome, where he gained his Licentiate and Doctorate in Sacred Theology. He was ordained there on 23rd December 1950.

After working in the British Isles he returned to Rome in 1954 as Inter in Philosphy to the English College, and was Professor of Philosophy at Beda College, Rome from 1957 to 1960.

Between 1966 and 1977 he was director of an ecumenical and pastoral centre at Wetherby, the first of its kind in Europe, which made a great impact on the ecumenical scene. In 1968, Michael Buckley was appointed Roman Catholic Religious Advisor to Yorkshire Television and still appears on many of their religious programmes.

Pope Paul VI appointed him to the Vatican Secretariat for Promoting Christian Unity, a position he held for five years from 1968, and he has continued this work through the Maranatha Community for reconciliation in Northern Ireland.

Monsignor Buckley has been Parish Priest of St Joseph's Church, Tadcaster, Yorkshire, but is now working full-time in the healing ministry.

Michael Buckley, D. D.

Let Peace Disturb You

*Insights into essential
Gospel words*

Collins
FOUNT PAPERBACKS

First published by Fount Paperbacks, London in 1985
Second impression February 1987

Copyright © Michael Buckley 1985

Made and printed in Great Britain by
William Collins Sons & Co. Ltd, Glasgow

To
Maranatha

Contents

Introduction

There are many "essential" gospel words without which the Gospel of Jesus Christ is stripped of its real meaning. These essential words are all so interrelated that the understanding of one involves a greater understanding of the others. The meaning of these words is grasped only through personal Christian experience when we attempt to live out in our lives the implications of the *full* Christian Gospel. Too often we only grasp their peripheral secular understanding because the gospel significance of the words is hidden like a jewel of great price which we have to discover for ourselves through events in our lives. Only those who have searched deeply and found for themselves the pearl of rare price can share their common joy and experience. Otherwise the words remain letters on a page and are not "lived" or "living" words.

The Gospel is not only Jesus' lived experience, it is ours as well when we take his life style and, measuring it against his words, try to live it in our daily lives. What he did gave authenticity and depth to what he said. He not only talked about poverty; he was poor. He told us to take up our cross daily and follow him, but not before he took up his own cross and died for our sake. He was able to tell us that we were to live one day at a time and not worry about the future only because he surrendered his whole life moment by moment to his Father. We were to be obedient to the Father because Jesus had been obedient unto death. He gave words a new dimension and they became essential gospel words bearing within themselves the secret of the Christian life. His way of life must be ours as well if we are to understand the true meaning of his message for us.

"Obedience", "poverty", "simplicity", "peace", "suffering", "trust", "love", "forgiveness", "prayer", "healing" are some of the many essential gospel words. In analysing any one of them we probe deeper into the meaning of the others. We will never understand "poverty" in all its fullness unless we are prepared to be "obedient" to the Father's will whatever the circumstances in which we are placed. We will never know "peace" until we "forgive" our enemies. I have called this book *Let Peace Disturb You*, but I could have inserted any other essential gospel word in the title and the result would have been the same. They are different aspects of the one Gospel message. All essential gospel words disturb us and yet are for our peace.

The Gospel that is not lived through experience is meaningless. Essential gospel words are experiential. It is easy to talk about poverty when you are rich, or about peace when you live in a comfortable, secure situation! The Gospel as a lived experience is disturbing about every aspect of our lives. It throws a question mark across the fabric of our lives and disturbs our *status quo*. Unless we know what they mean to us through experience then essential gospel words such as "forgiveness" and "trust" remain words and ideals rather than the teaching of Jesus which we must follow, otherwise the meaning of essential gospel words and the dynamic life style of Jesus will remain hidden from our eyes, no matter how long we study the Bible. They are words in a book about the life of someone who died two thousand years ago.

The Gospel is to be lived in its *fullness*. Only the Holy Spirit can unfold its message for us. He shows us that the keys which unlock the Gospel for us have to be forged in our own lives under his guidance and power. Each key is to be cut according to the pattern of the life style of Jesus. The keys are the essential gospel words. This book contains but a few. I hope that, like me, in reading it you will not only discover the true meaning of peace but experience it in your life.

1

Being Disturbed By The Gospel

Peacemaking

The peace of Christ disturbed my life. Let me explain. As a Christian I want to live in peace but peace is a strange word with many meanings. All religion is supposed to bring peace to its followers, and the Christian religion is no exception. Followers of every religion, worship in various ways the God of peace. However, Christians are offered a unique form of peace unequalled by other religions. It is a peace which is at the same time fulfilling and disturbing. Jesus, the Son of God, is our peacemaker and his gift to us is his peace. "Peace I bequeath to you, my own peace I give you, a peace the world cannot give, this is my gift to you" (John 14:27). Christ is our peace, says St Paul, because "by his cross he has restored peace between us and reconciled us to God" (Ephesians 2:14–15). As Christians if we receive Christ's peace then we are, or should be, at peace within ourselves because we are at peace with God and with each other. But strangely enough Christians, even among themselves, are not noted for their peacefulness. History in fact has underlined the opposite. Why is this so? The reason is because they have never discovered for themselves the true gospel meaning of peace. They shortcircuited its meaning for the sake of quick returns.

At first sight "peace" seems a straightforward, simple word. We all say we want peace, but we are not at peace. Why? We are peacelovers but not necessarily peacemakers.

We are not prepared to receive Christ's peace into our lives because we are afraid of its disturbing influence. He made peace between us and God, established peaceful relations between all peoples, but only through his death on the Cross. On his part this is the price of his peace which he offers to us. I too have to pay the price of Christian peace in my life. I am growing in my understanding of what Jesus meant by peace, and how I should prepare myself to receive it, as I grow in my Christian faith. To understand the meaning of peace is to understand the life of Jesus, and to enter into a deep appreciation of his suffering reflected by events in my own life. If I want his peace I have to pay the price of following him no matter what the cost. The quality of his peace in my life depends on the price I pay for following him.

Peace is at the heart of the Christian Gospel. *Shalom* (peace) was also at the centre of Jewish belief and practice. Yet Jeremias castigated the Jewish priests for their false understanding of what it meant. "Peace! Peace! they say, but there is no peace. They should be ashamed of their abominable deeds" (Jeremias 6:14). Have we Christians misunderstood the meaning of peace and fallen into the same trap? I think we have.

As Christians we speak too lightly of peace, forgetting that its inner meaning is as demanding as the Christian Gospel itself. The Gospel takes a lifetime of meditation and action. It is like a film of our lives which is unfolded moment by moment. So the inner meaning of peace takes us through the depths and shallows, the joy and pain of our pilgrimage in search of the Holy Grail of peace. Peace, as St Ephraim says, is like every word which is of the essence of the Christian Gospel:

> Lord, who can grasp all the wealth of just one of your words? What we understand in the Bible is much less

> than what we leave behind, like thirsty people who
> drink from a fountain. For your word has many
> shades of meaning, just as those who study it have
> many different points of view. You have coloured
> your words with many hues so that each person who
> studies it can see in it what he loves. You have hidden
> many treasures in your word so that each one of us is
> enriched as we meditate on it.

We all differ in our interpretation of peace depending upon
our interpretation of the Gospel, and how we see it reflected in our own lives and circumstances.

The peace Jesus offers us is unique because it is a peace in
the midst of conflict. In fact it seems the opposite of peace.
He told his followers, "Do not suppose that I have come to
bring peace to the earth: it is not peace I have come to
bring, but a sword. For I have come to set a man against his
father, a daughter against her mother, a daughter-in-law
against her mother-in-law" (Matthew 10:34–35). Jesus
offers us the internal peace of a good conscience, often at
the expense of external peace, the kind of peace the world
holds precious. It is a peace born of the pain of misunderstanding, rejection, even imprisonment. When he said that
he came not to bring peace but the sword, it was not his
intention to cause conflict but he saw it as a consequence of
the absoluteness of his teaching on peace which would cut
across people's lives like a sword. He was reminding his
followers that he was not coming to bring peace and quiet,
but on the contrary he was offering them gospel peace,
which would involve them in a great deal of suffering and
misunderstanding as well as conflict within themselves.
Peace will always be won only at the greatest price.

What is the "sword" Jesus has come to bring his
followers? It is the Gospel, God's living word with its
sharp cutting edge of truth about man and his destiny. "The

word of God is something alive and active: it cuts like any double-edged sword but more finely: it can slip through the place where the soul is divided from the spirit, or joints from the marrow; it can judge the secret emotions and thoughts" (Hebrews 4:12). The Gospel of Jesus disturbs us deep within ourselves because it is the divine surgeon's scalpel, which penetrates to the real source of our spiritual disease. It is like a Caesarean operation allowing us to be born. Just as a medical operation is painful but necessary for life when we are ill, so the first condition of being open to the Gospel, and the ultimate peace it offers, is to submit ourselves to God's will for us however painful it may be. For example, we will only really believe in the Resurrection as a true gospel fact in our lives when we hand over our bereavement of a loved one to God's loving care. The pain of loss, while still within us, is submerged in the Resurrection. Just as in a strange way we cling to our bereavement, so in a sense we do not want to undergo the pain which the operation of letting the Gospel come alive in us brings. We cling to what we know and what we have, and so we are tempted to live with the disease of sin within us which will ultimately erode and destroy our full vision of the Christian life. We settle for second best. We opt for the pain-killing drug which is labelled "peace" but only brings temporary respite.

We grow in our awareness of Christian peace as we allow the Gospel to be our rule of life. The Gospel demands total commitment; its peace costs nothing less than everything. Jesus himself asked his followers to leave everything and everyone for his sake because this was the only way to gospel peace. The way of his peace is the way of his Cross. As a result of living by his teaching many of his disciples met violent deaths; and yet this rejection by society is precisely what he offered them when they first chose to follow him: "Beware of men: they will hand you over to sanhedrins and scourge you in their synagogues. You will be dragged before governors and kings for my sake, to bear witness before them and the pagans. . . . Brother will betray brother to death, and the father his child; children will rise against their parents and have them put to death. You will be hated by all men on account of my name; but the man who stands firm to the end will be saved. If they persecute you in one town, take refuge in the next; and if they persecute you in that, take refuge in another" (Matthew 10:17–18, 21–23).

Apart from physical pain rejection by one's own family is one of the greatest suffering many Christians who have given their lives to Christ have had to endure. Yet it opened up their souls, minds, hearts and emotions to the Gospel of Peace and forgiveness like a sword which cut them in two. It set them free even though they were deeply hurt in the process. Jesus, message of total following of his teaching may also cut us off from our friends when they, for whatever reason, reject our Christian way of life and our concept of peace. This shows the enormity of the price of living out the Gospel to the full that people like St Francis of Assisi had to pay, and which is still being paid today by truly committed Christians. Their total Christian commitment to the Gospel of Jesus in their search for peace involves them in a complete upheaval of their lives. The one thing they cannot be false to is the Gospel. It brings them both peace and disturbance in perpetual conflict. If I think that being a Christian does not involve me in rejection then I do not know what the Gospel of Peace really means. This rejection reaches down to touch those from whom we would least expect it even within the institutions which we hold dear. Even in the Church we do not speak the same language of peace.

Peace, therefore, for Jesus has overtones of conflict. When he offers peace to us what he in fact offers is his way of life. For him peace is total obedience to God his Father. He saw peace as the union of his will with that of his Father, and it was in this union of wills that the essence of his peace lay. Being obedient to God the Father is never easy. It was not so for Jesus, but as long as he was at peace with God and within his own soul then all was well, no matter how violent the situation in which he found himself. His peace was opposed to the kind of peace offered by the world. He told his followers: "Do not be afraid of those who kill the body but cannot kill the soul; fear him rather who can destroy both body and soul in hell" (Matthew 10:28). Many of us in seeking the world's peace destroy our peace of soul. And yet St Teresa reminds us of the need for true peace of soul:

> Let nothing disturb thee,
> Let nothing affright thee,
> All things are changing,
> God only is changeless.
> Patient endurance attaineth to all things,
> Alone, God sufficeth.

The Gospel of Jesus in my experience does not confine itself to external disturbances like the loss of money or friends, but penetrates to the very depths of our souls. Jesus demands in his Father's name our total service and unconditional following of him if we want his peace. His search for peace within himself was threatened by suffering and made him cry out in the garden: "My soul is sorrowful to the point of death," and on the Cross: "My God, my God, why have you deserted me?" (Matthew 27:46). This disturbance within ourselves, threatening even our souls, is the ante-chamber to peace. The pain of loss of the presence of God within us, even for a time, when we feel abandoned and alone, is a most disturbing and frightening experience. I have been through that valley of darkness. Yet it was in fact for me a very special grace from God because I now know that through the disturbances it caused within me I grew more fully in peace. The feeling of abandonment tested my faith and love just as surely as Jesus was tempted in the Garden. When I came through it I experienced something of the strength which Jesus felt when his temptations in the desert were over. It was like coming out of a dark tunnel and standing on a mountain top breathing in air which tasted of champagne. Peace comes when the battle with compromise is over and we can take our rest, even if only for a short time, because the world will not let us go. Its attractions remain and we have to fight against them.

Once I began to understand that for Jesus peace was a way of life and a quality deep within his soul, which dominated his every word and action, I had to ask myself the question, "What does Jesus' peace mean to me as a Christian?" Is it a word which trips lightly off my tongue because as a Christian I am expected to be a peaceful person who is "all for peace", or is it a lived gospel experience in whose cause I have to suffer before I can find peace for myself? Is it purely negative – like the absence of trouble – or is it the most positive element dominating my life? Does gospel peace push further back the frontiers of the vision of my destiny as a Christian disciple, or do I settle simply for peace and quiet? Do I read the Gospel of Jesus as an esoteric, romantic story of an idealist striving for peace, or do I see it as his life come alive in my own everyday experiences? Does peace conjure up carpet slippers and a cosy fire, or is it the ultimate dynamic in my life, driving me forward when others tell me I have travelled far enough and that I have done enough for peace? Is it perpetual conformity to rule or standing up and being counted? Am I to be the prophet, or the blind, unthinking conformist? Does it make me be perfectly honest with my eyes on the

Gospel, or encourage me to say the "right thing" with my eyes on the main chance? What price, in fact, am I prepared to pay for daring to call myself a Christian?

Christian peace, I repeat, is a lived gospel experience. We can only talk meaningfully about it with someone who has a similar experience. Peace is not a theory but a way of life. If we have not experienced the hardships of apartheid, or been the victims of an oppressive regime, then it is hard to talk of peace with justice to those who have. We can only appreciate to some degree what they mean by it, and learn from them. It is only when we find ourselves in similar situations that we begin to understand its deeper meaning.

It is from the Third World today that prophets are proclaiming the Gospel of Peace. They are suffering in its cause because the circumstances in which they find themselves threaten the dignity and destiny of mankind. In the West our concept of peace is limited and limiting. As a rule we live too contentedly outside the fuller meaning of the Gospel, until its message is brought home to us through a crisis in our own lives. It is perhaps only then for the first time that we begin to understand the meaning of Christ's words to us: "a peace that the world cannot give, this is my gift to you" (John 14:27). These words relate to our experience in a new, incisive way once we allow them to change the pattern of our lives. Up till then they are just words in a book which we have repeated so often that they have become well-worn clichés.

Let me give you an example from my own life of how I came to a deeper appreciation of what Christ meant by peace. For many long years I had campaigned against the odds for peace with justice for both Protestants and Catholics in Northern Ireland. Very few understood what I meant by peace even amongst my closest friends. Northern Ireland was then, as it is now, a political and ecclesiastical minefield. Everyone had his own solution. Most of them wanted peace for all but if there was not enough peace to go round then peace enough for their own group, much as they regretted the lack of it for others. Things came to a head in my life in 1976 during the time of the massive, emotional marches of the Peace People of Northern Ireland. Their response to the physical violence in their lives touched a part of me which yearned to end all bigotry, hatred and violence which plagued the people I had come to love and serve.

A few months after the start of the Peace Movement I convened the inaugural meeting of peace workers from all over England, Scotland and Wales, and it was held at the pastoral and ecumenical centre of which I was in charge. It was during that weekend conference that my own life was disturbed. I began to discover in my search for some kind of peace in Northern Ireland what gospel peace really meant. This is how it came about. During Mass that weekend when it came to the Sign of Peace I saluted the Peace People of Northern Ireland with the words, "May the peace of Christ thoroughly *disturb* you." I was speaking to them of their search for a just peace both for themselves and for their troubled land, but the Spirit took me at my words. He wanted my peace too, and so the Spirit disturbed me and not them! They were hoping to find peace among the bombs and bullets of towns and cities in Northern Ireland, and I was too secure in my pastoral centre, tucked away in a lovely Yorkshire valley, to talk to them of peace in a meaningful way.

It is easy to preach on poverty when you are rich, or on peace when you are in a comfortable situation. Within a fortnight I had to leave the pastoral centre at Wood Hall which I had hoped would become a national peace centre, and was forced to look again at the Gospel in order to understand what Christ meant by the words "Peace I bequeath to you, my own peace I give you" (John 14:27). My

21

inner peace was shattered for a time, but now I am dis-
covering day by day that the true price of Christian peace is
the same as that which I have to pay for living out the full
Gospel of Jesus Christ in all sorts of other ways. The
shattering experience of that weekend changed my whole
Christian life. I smile now when I hear people say, "Of
course, I am all for peace", because in point of fact what
they are really saying is, "I don't want to be disturbed in
my comfortable life in which no one is allowed to rock the
boat." It saddens me, on reflection, that I too was like that
because I did not understand what the Gospel meant by
peace, and so I liked to preach it rather than live it. It made
me "feel good" and preserved my "caring Christian" image.
The Gospel that is not lived through experience is
meaningless. It is a string of words which do not compel
assent and involvement. We can only talk of peace in the
measure that we have paid the price to make its kingdom
come on earth.

Now through that single experience with the Peace
People I have discovered that the Gospel is disturbing not
only about peace but about every aspect of my Christian
life. It turns my life upside down. I am not a pessimist or
cynic yet I believe the world is a sham. The Gospel shows it
up for what it is, and once I am prepared to believe then the
Gospel is as disturbing as the apathy and sham it has to
overcome. For me peacemaking through reconciliation is of
the essence of the Gospel and just as challenging. It has
become, for me at least, the most explosive commodity in
our world, which unfortunately careful, diplomatic Christians store away in a safe place. Like politicians in a power
game they opt for the well-trodden paths of the world so
that their lives are a maze of compromises rather than the
straight, narrow road of the Gospel. They talk of peace but
there is no peace because they preach and live by its
counterfeit. Peace comes too easy to them. They contribute

to the world's *status quo* of violence and injustice without consciously intending to, because this is the end result of their counterfeit of what Jesus meant by peace.

In a sense I do not condemn them because they have no experience of the opposite which might have become a crisis, a growth point, in their lives such as happened in the life of Archbishop Romero, the martyr for peace. They see peace in their terms of reference of the Gospel; Romero saw it in his. Since my involvement with the Peace People of Northern Ireland I can appreciate much more personally the ideals for which Archbishop Romero lived and died. For me, peace as offered by Jesus is an invitation from him to share in the pain and misunderstanding he suffered at the hands of his own people. Once I commit myself open-endedly to the Gospel of Christ then I have to be prepared for anything. His spirit will lead me into a new under-standing of truth, and his Gospel – whether it be of peace, forgiveness, reconciliation, love or any other essential Christian virtue – will always disturb me.

I am not saying that I am better than other Christians in my understanding of peace, but rather that my own narrow vision of it has been widened through God's grace and my involvement with the situation in Northern Ireland. But even still there are times when my vision of peace is dulled, and I am tempted to settle for less than Christ would have done, or have me do. It is at times like these that I cannot understand my own behaviour: "I fail to carry out the things I want to do and I find myself doing the very things I hate" (Romans 7:15).

The reason this happens, and the source of our various limited visions of what is meant by the word "peace", is due to the consequences of sin. We are divided within ourselves. We are divided between our "Christian self", which wants true peace and our "selfish self", which wants power, recognition, "peace and comfort" and all the paraphernalia of a fallen world. Rather than allow ourselves to be disturbed by the full Gospel of Jesus we settle for a superficial understanding of what it means to be a Christian, and thus sow the seeds of our own ultimate lack of Christian fulfilment. We take the easy way out and turn our backs on those parts of the teaching of Jesus which could disturb us. We are selective rather than committed Christians when it comes to following the Gospel. Like the Devil, we can quote scripture for our purpose.

We do not do this deliberately, and would loudly protest that this is not true, but we are modern Pharisees who have a blind spot when it comes to judging our own behaviour in the light of the Gospel. Our vision of Jesus is blurred. The effect of sin on us is that although our "Christian self" wants to follow Jesus and experience his peaceful presence in our lives, nevertheless our "selfish self" is afraid of the price we will have to pay. In the final analysis we have to choose between Jesus and the world in our lives. We cannot have both. Make no mistake about it, the materialistic world, whatever our commitment to our churches, has a hypnotic pull on our "selfish self" with its false sense of values. Our motivation is mixed because our commitment is not total. The "Christian self" is often overwhelmed by the "selfish self", and so the Gospel of Peace dies the slow death of suffocation in the desert we have made of our lives.

Even when we do honestly try to live out the full Gospel of Peace in our lives, we discover that it always remains a constant struggle because we still cling to the "selfish self". Despite Jesus' promise of peace, our "selfish self" resists any attempt to dislodge its firm hold on our lives. Even despite our Christian conviction that we must die to the "selfish self" in order to live true to ourselves as God wants us to do, we automatically resist any disturbance of our comfort because there is still a changing and a dying to be undergone within us if we want to live the full Christian

Gospel. Even when we think we have accepted the Gospel into our lives, there is still a struggle, and we are instinctively afraid of change and death. So as Christians we are "at peace" and "disturbed" within ourselves at the same time. "At peace" because we are attempting to be true to the teaching of Jesus, and "disturbed" because although we are growing in the fullness of the gospel peace, and growth involves the pain of change, we also want an easier life. The Gospel and sin are in conflict within us, and we are afraid of the pain involved. The scene of the battlefield is within us, and no one likes that. Our peace is a constant battle where ground so dearly won can be easily lost when we relax our concentration and watchfulness.

Thomas Merton sums up the inward Christian disturbance and struggle for peace: "Although God wanted life to be a pure consciousness of love and peace," he writes, "it is actually a fierce struggle, because in our actual human existence life is the agony of a love which fears to accept itself; self-affirmation and self-negation at one and the same time." For Thomas Merton there is the paradoxical tension between the affirmation of the "Christian self" locked in combat with the negation of the "selfish self", so that we come alive to our "Christian self" in relation to our dying to our "selfish self". We are afraid to love ourselves as Christians, afraid to accept the obligations as well as the privileges of being chosen by God as the brothers and sisters of his Son.

Yet peace is the birthright and mission of all Christians. The question remains as to how I can be sure that I have found this peace with its paradoxical disturbance. I may be disturbed within myself but not because of my living out the Gospel. On the contrary, my pain may come from my conscience telling me that I am not being or doing what I should be or do. *I have therefore, in the final analysis, to trust my peace to Christ.* Thomas Merton sums up the dilemma:

The fact that I think that I am following your will
  does not mean that I am actually doing so.
But I believe that the desire to please you
  does in fact please you,
And I hope I have that desire
  in all that I am doing.
I hope that I will never do anything apart
  from that desire.
And I know that if I do this,
  you will lead me by the right road though I may know
  nothing about it.
Therefore will I trust you always though I
  may seem lost and in the shadow of death.

The path to peace is for us the incarnation of Jesus' life in us. The characteristics of Jesus' peace were many, and in this book I have selected a few, such as his unselfish love for friend and foe alike and all that this involved; his rejection of the world's false worship of power and privilege, his identification with the poorest and humblest in society; his use of creative periods of silence for prayer, and total acceptance of suffering and death as God's will for him, and his healing and forgiving ministry dedicated to others. In all this he uncovered for us the full meaning of peace. Jesus, in the fullest sense of the word, was in fact the only perfectly peaceful man this world has ever known.

With the example of Jesus' life before us we know by faith that the peace of the Gospel is a vision which we have glimpsed from the top of the mountain of experience. The Gospel lights up our experience and expresses it in Christian terms and actions. Once we have seen it we are no longer content to remain where we are, but become in a true, peaceful sense "restless" because we have been given fresh courage and inspiration to climb higher mountains so that our vision of peace may be clearer.

2

Growing Through Suffering

Compassion

If I want to be at peace then I must be prepared to suffer. Why? Because suffering is of the essence of the Christian Gospel. Without it I shall never know deep inner peace, and yet suffering seems the opposite of peace. It challenges me, and all too often I find that my response to it in gospel terms is lacking in commitment. I know from experience that it is the silent language of the Christian Gospel of Peace, and yet it still baffles me. It is a paradox. Suffering disturbs my peace and yet it is for my peace. It presents me not so much with the abstract problem of pain, but with its presence right in the centre of my own life. I am naïve enough to claim to have some understanding of it, but when it is no longer "something out there affecting other people" but has invaded my own life, then I am not so sure. In my own small way I have had to learn from experience to face it and to trust that it comes from a loving God whom Jesus tells me is my Father. This is how the Gospel of Jesus looks on suffering. Jesus himself laid down the conditions for those who wished to become his disciples: "If anyone wants to be a follower of mine, let him renounce himself and take up his cross and follow me" (Matthew 16:24). All suffering, when used creatively in union with Jesus' submission to his Father's will, has a purpose for my spiritual growth and inner peace. Isn't that what St Paul meant when he wrote, "We know that by turning everything to their good God co-operates with all those who love him, with all those that he has called according to his purpose?" (Romans 8:23).

If I am honest with myself, and how difficult that is, then I have to admit that, because it involves all types of suffering life as a Christian is neither easy nor predictable. There have been times in my life when suffering was so paramount and inner peace seemed so far away that I have wondered if ever I would find it again. The suffering I experienced then, which I know was not self-inflicted, threw my Christian vision of life off balance. Yet on hindsight I have gradually discovered through a painful process that it was in these very times of personal pain that God was in fact calling me to deepen my faith and trust in him. Such suffering, when I took it and offered it to God my Father in obedience, was the source of a peace I would not otherwise have known. The real source of my growth as a Christian was through a situation over which I had no control. The instruments of my growth were unwittingly used by God to make me surrender my life totally to Him, and to no one else.

In times of suffering, when I find it hard to see through the clouds of doubt because my spiritual awareness is numbed, and I am too conscious of the pain I am suffering, I invariably turn to the Gospel of Jesus' life for inspiration. I know that since "God did not spare his own Son he will not refuse anything he can give" (Romans 8:32). Jesus reminds me at these times by the example of his own life that it is through suffering that I can grow in inner peace, and a closer following of him. So when I want to understand my own sufferings, and how they help me to grow in peace I take a look at some of his, and what they did for his peace. Now I know what is meant by the words "no evil will I fear".

When Jesus was thirty years old he had the desert experience. It happened when he went to John the Baptist to be baptized. "No sooner had he come up out of the water than he saw the heavens torn apart and the Spirit, like a dove, descending on him. And a voice came from heaven, 'You are my Son, the Beloved; my favour rests on you' " (Mark 1:10–11). It was natural to expect that Jesus would be left in peace for a long period to enjoy the special sign of his Father's love given in such a perfect setting by the banks of the Jordan, but it was not to be because God's ways are just simply not ours. Jesus immediately went into the desert where he had to endure many frightening temptations.

What was the purpose of these temptations and how do we reconcile them with God's declared love for his Son? Does God vacillate from love to apparent punishment so that he seems to enjoy watching the suffering of those whom he loves? Suffering is, in fact, a growth point for our good and we must not imagine that God himself places any value in suffering as an end in itself. If that were so he would not be our Father. St Thérèse of Lisieux reminds us: "Never do our sufferings make God happy but they are necessary for us. He sends us sorrow while as it were turning away his face." So it was with Jesus. He grew in the desert through the trial of his temptations, and emerged with the determination and power to begin his public ministry precisely because he used his suffering properly, and allowed it to mould him even more into the man his Father wanted him to be. "Jesus *with the power of the Spirit*, returned to Galilee, and his reputation spread throughout the countryside. He taught in their synagogues and everyone praised him" (Luke 4:14).

The suffering of the temptations was a blessing for Jesus' growth; after it he was a changed man. No one will ever fully understand the hardships and trials which he endured in those forty days and nights alone in that wild place, but it was there that the history of the world was being shaped and crystallized in this man of destiny. All of the sufferings of Jesus, each in its own way, fitted him for his mission. They prepared him to receive the power of the Spirit. He shows me by his example that I too will suffer but that these times of trial and temptation, if I use them properly, are a necessary preparation for a profound change in the direction of my life. If I am to live the full Christian life and grow through all the trials which test me then I shall remember that God is still with me as my Father, and, as with Jesus, when temptation is over he will send his Spirit to help me grow and mature in full Christian peace. I may believe this in faith because faith may be my only support from falling into despair and self-pity. Suffering is a very disturbing way to find inner peace but it is often the only one. This is the mystery and anomaly of our Christian faith. I write this not as a platitude but as something I learned in the school of life.

The desert, too, is a symbolic place of desolation where before God I come face to face with myself and, through my trials, grow in inner peace through my Christian conviction and sense of purpose in life. Jesus needed the desert with its temptations, and no chance of escape, in order to be better equipped for his mission of peace for the world. Is it any wonder that the desert, the symbolic place of loneliness, is called by the Arabs "the Garden of Allah"?

But nowhere is the growth aspect of suffering more clearly shown than at the end of Jesus' life when he suffered in the garden of Gethsemane. His spiritual growth in peace was such that he conquered within himself that night his human fear of his passion and death. "Then Jesus came with them to a small estate called Gethsemane; and he said to his disciples, 'Stay here while I go over there to pray.' He took Peter and the two sons of Zebedee with him. And sadness came over him, and great distress. Then he said to them, 'My soul is sorrowful to the point of death. Wait here and keep awake with me.' And going on a little further he fell on his face and prayed. 'My Father,' he said, 'if it is possible, let this cup pass me by. Nevertheless, let it be as you, not I, would have it' " (Matthew 26:36–39). This was his moment of crisis and truth, when his own preaching of "dying to live", and total surrender to his Father would be put to the test. The force directing his life, his love of his Father, which was nourished by the temptations in the desert, was now finding its ultimate fulfilment in the Garden of Sorrows. His real trial of himself began and ended in Gethsemane; what the soldiers and his own Jewish priests and people would do on the morrow was of little consequence. Caiaphas, Annas, Herod and Pilate were mere bit players in the drama of Jesus' use of suffering within himself. Jesus said, "This is the hour of darkness" because he freely chose it to be that way, and so the man in the desert under trial by temptation who was to become the world's missioner, was in the great moment of crisis totally at peace within himself. During his subsequent shameful trial, passion and crucifixion his union with his Father in prayer showed him what his suffering was all about, and so setting the pain of his passion against his love for his Father, he came to his decision. When he rose up from the prayer in the garden he had a mysterious calmness, courage and peace about him which baffled everyone. Why? Because he had faced up to the ultimate in suffering – his own death – and his peace of soul was something which was with him all through his trial and passion. He had been disturbed in the process – "my soul is sorrowful to the point of death" – but now that he was prepared to pay the ultimate price, he possessed a deep inner peace which no one could take away from him.

So through the Gospel Jesus tells me, in the desert, the garden and the cross, that I must learn to use suffering creatively if I am to find peace of soul. The test of love has always been what we are prepared to endure for its sake.

Suffering, because of our love of God our Father, is the hallmark of people of faith who offer their lives to him as the only thing of value that is left to them because they have already given him everything else. This is the stuff of which martyrs are made. It may well be that in certain situations involving suffering we may be denied the comfort of friends, or any solace whatsoever, but we know that God is still our Father who wants our peace, and he will show us the way out of the valley of darkness in which we have found ourselves. In the meantime we have to possess our souls in peace trusting that God as a Father will provide the answer.

Our faith which is put to the test by suffering brings us a peace which we would never have known without it, and which we can explain only to those with a similar experience. An insight into Psalm 23 may help us in times of distress:

> In pastures green?
> Not always; sometimes He
> Who knoweth best, in kindness leadeth me
> In weary ways where heavy shadows be;
> Out of the sunshine warm and soft and bright,
> Out of the sunshine into darkest night,
> I oft would faint with sorrow and affright,
> Only for this I know He holds my hand
> So whether in a green or desert land
> I trust Him, though I do not understand.
>
> And by still waters?
> No, not always so;
> Oft–time the heavy tempests round me blow,
> And over my soul the waves and billows go,
> But when the storm beats loudest and I cry
> Aloud for help, the Master standeth by

And whispers to my soul, "Lo! It is I".
Above the tempest wild I hear Him say,
"Beyond this darkness lies the perfect day,
In every path of thine I lead the way."

So, whether on the hilltop high and fair
I dwell, or in the sunless valley where
The shadows lie – what matter? He is there.
Yea, more than this: where'er the pathway lead,
He gives to me no helpless broken reed,
But his own hand sufficient for my need.
So where He leadeth I can safely go;
And in the blest hereafter I shall know
Why, in His wisdom, He hath led me so.

Jesus himself knew only too well the weight which sufferings impose on the human soul, and yet it is the very pain of suffering itself which lights up our lives and is the only means which often makes us face up to our real selves. We may get some understanding of its spiritual value when we realize that the deepest inner peace is born out of pain. We come to birth through the pain of our mothers and as we grow older we will perhaps realize that every pain which we use creatively is for our peace and growth. I know from experience that there is no growth in inner peace where there is not a corresponding suffering through which we discover ourselves and deepen our faith in God as a loving Father. Jesus, in all his suffering, reminds us that our trust in God as a loving Father who will not cause us an unnecessary tear is indispensable for our inner peace. Such trust is not to be regarded by us an an ointment to heal our wounds or as a solace to comfort our souls, but must be seen as set into the heart of suffering and our spiritual growth. One gives meaning to the other. Suffering which is not creative is of its nature destructive.

To suffer creatively is, for the Christian, what we call *compassion*, a linking of our pain with that of Jesus himself. It unites us with his work of reconciliation, and is compassionate because it means entering as Jesus did into other people's problems and sufferings. Mary Craig, in her excellent book *Blessings*, sums up exactly what this important aspect of suffering means: "Our tragedy is not that we suffer but that we waste suffering. We waste the opportunity of growing into compassion."

Let me give you an example of compassion. I preached a mission in Rhodesia to African Sisters some years ago, and I was apprehensive as to its outcome, mainly because of the cultural barriers between them and myself. My fears were unfounded. From the outset the mission was a great success, and I say this without any pretence of boasting because it was obvious to everyone else and to me that the Holy Spirit was at work in a most tangible way. When the week's mission was over I asked the Superior if I could visit the sick Sisters, and there in a cubicle I found the source of its success. She was a young sister in her early thirties who had already undergone fifteen operations, and was bedridden for most of her religious life. She told me that for a whole year, ever since she heard I was first coming, she had offered up her prayers and sufferings for the mission. Her pain during the week, she said, was the worst she ever experienced, and yet there was a smile on her lips and peace in her eyes. I have never experienced in my life such joy and peace in any individual, nor such obvious witness of the power of the presence of the Holy Spirit. Through the wonderful surrender of her illness every moment of that mission I knew that it was the Spirit of Jesus in her which was working marvels for us all. I shall never forget what she did for her community and me. In her sick bed, where she lived out her baptismal commitment she led the fullest life I have ever encountered because she shared it with God.

She was full of compassion as she offered up her pain for her Sisters in union with the agony and passion of her Lord.

Most of us are still in the area of doing our best to accept suffering, never mind being compassionate as the African Sister was. It is wrong to minimize the effect pain has on us as Christians, and to pretend, as some Pentecostals do, that we are "above all that". A "born again" Christian is just as afraid of pain as anyone else. I "naturally" fear pain because of what it will do to me in my "selfish self", and yet without it there can be little growth in my "Christian self". Suffering involves me in change and a "dying" which I resent because in my body and spirit I am instinctively afraid of change and death just as Jesus was. There is no point in the grain of wheat dying unless it produces fresh ears of wheat in the process. Winter, for example, finds its fulfilment in spring and harvest time because all death in nature is a precondition of life. My suffering, therefore, has meaning only in the Resurrection of Jesus in which I share through baptism. More and more I treasure the text of St Paul when he writes of our Christian belief in the meaning and effect of baptism: "When we were baptized in Christ Jesus we were baptized in his death, so that as Christ was raised from the dead by the Father's glory, we too might live a new life" (Romans 6:3-4). When I suffer creatively then I share in Christ's resurrection and victory.

For many years now I cannot find true inner peace, nor appreciate the hidden value of any suffering, unless I personally see in it the pattern of Christ's Resurrection. This does not mean just the resurrection of my physical body but of the Resurrection at work in the suffering I am experiencing *now*. Suffering otherwise is pointless. It is one thing to accept this at an intellectual level when life is calm, and quite another when suffering challenges me. The resurrection is the true dawn in which we walk as Christians when the fever of suffering has broken, and our selfish clinging to ourselves has been conquered. I have to remind myself constantly of this when suffering comes, and it is never easy.

It is here again that the Gospel, with its full meaning of the Resurrection, helps me and the story of Christ's life inspires me. Jesus had submitted to the ultimate in suffering, the "operation of death", and with "Peace be to you" as the password on his lips he walked out into the daylight leaving behind his bandages of suffering in the tomb. After his Resurrection and triumph he brings his message of gospel peace to the world through his followers who are now an Easter people. He tells us that from the day of his own Resurrection onwards no Christian is to be anxious about any "dying" since even physical death has lost its sting. I may worry that I will not be able to endure future sufferings, for example, if I am told that I have a terminal disease. Yet if I believe in the resurrection after physical death, which is the ultimate in this life, then why should I be afraid to believe that he will raise me up from every other intermediate form of dying involved in suffering? If he heals me of death then he will heal me of every other form of suffering. I believe that the risen Jesus with his message of peace is in every difficult and painful situation, in which I have found or will find myself, and through my belief in this I am prepared to die a physical death if this is necessary in my search for inner gospel peace. It was always so with the Christian martyrs from the earliest times, and suffering will always be a form of dying in order to live. The inner peace we possess as Christians, therefore, in every situation however calamitous, is the peace of the Resurrection. With the Risen Jesus, I can conquer every form of death through my Christian baptism. If I did not believe this then my life is meaningless and the power game is right.

Suffering is destructive of our inner peace when it cuts us off from other people. We feel lost and alone. The real problem in all my sufferings, however, will always remain myself and my damaged way of looking at my situation, which I tend to get out of focus. It is in times like these that the risen Jesus assures me of his help: "Come to me all you who labour and are heavy burdened and I will give you rest" (Matthew 11:28). Jesus is the most compassionate person in our world, and when I learn to share my sufferings with him he will take them into the heart of his Resurrection. It is in, and with, him that I find peace. He invites me every moment of every day to walk with him through suffering to peace, and even to be ready, like Simon of Cyrene, to share his load. Caryll Houselander, writing on the significance of Jesus allowing Simon to carry the Cross with him, says that "it means that no one is meant to suffer alone. No one is meant to carry his own cross without some other human being to help him. The pride which claims to be independent of human sympathy and practical help from others is unChristian. We are here to help one another, we are here to help Christ in one another." Our Maranatha Community helps us to share our lives deeply with one another so that *together* we can come to Christ for healing.

Far from sharing our problems with Christ or with one another, I have found after more than thirty years in the priestly ministry that many people suffer alone. Much of the suffering I have encountered in others is self-inflicted and pointless. Let me give you some examples. The woman who cannot tell her doctor what she believes is really wrong with her and so fills herself with pills for a disease she does not have; the young couple who do not talk to each other because they are afraid of losing face by owning up to their shortcomings, and no longer can say to each other "I love you" because they fail to say "I am sorry"; the youngster who becomes aggressive with his parents because he desperately wants to tell them what is eating him up inside; the person who puts up the calm exterior instead of being honest enough to say "I just can't cope anymore"; the widow who has been praised for being so brave yet all she needs to do is to break down and cry; the adolescent who goes to church every Sunday, which he knows is driving him further away from God, yet is too fearful not to go because of the reaction of his parents; the man who is afraid really to talk to his "boss" and hates himself for his cowardice; the wife who weeps tears on her pillow because she yearns to tell her husband that love means more than sex; the adolescent who has reached puberty and hides it from his parents who still treat him as a child; the cleric who is haunted by the dread that he has lost his faith and cannot trust anyone with his secret; the spouse who cannot tell the other of the unfaithfulness for which they cannot forgive themselves; the secret drinker or gambler who knows he is destroying himself yet sees no way out; the wife or husband who get themselves into a financial mess and dread the next post with its flood of bills.

These are but a few of the worries which haunt people, causing them to suffer unnecessarily, disturbing their inner peace of soul. In practically every case I have found that the root cause of people hiding their sufferings is that they do not trust "the other", whether it be God or people. This is because basically they are afraid that "the other" will not understand the problem, will leave them on their own to sort it out or, worse still, reject them. So they keep a stiff upper lip and all the while the tension within them builds up to breaking point. Yet we will continually be amazed to find how kind, understanding and compassionate those we love can be; if they are not, then they have a bigger problem in themselves than we could ever have! The nub of the question of how to find peace of mind and heart in the midst of suffering will always remain the amount of trustful sharing of ourselves we are prepared to make, and sharing is part and parcel of being a Christian. I have found in my healing ministry that people need to be released from fear so that they can share. Yet there are many Christians, even in prayer groups, who do not share at a deep level those things which affect their inner peace. I always talk out my sufferings and problems first with Jesus. I always find a peace and calm in this sharing which the world cannot give, and this helps me to face anything, come what may. Because I have shared with him I am able to share with others, and through this sharing (compassion) I have a faint glimmering of what Jesus meant when he said "my peace I give to you". If, for example, I talk to him about my sufferings and problems he makes me look at the Cross and then at the empty tomb, to remind me that all I suffer is part of his redeeming act for the whole world. When I allow suffering to disturb me Jesus adjusts the balance and calms the troubled waters: "Why are you afraid? Why is it you have no faith?" He carries my cross with me.

Sharing our life with the risen Jesus who knew what it was to conquer suffering in his own mind and body will help us to rise above all the pain of the world in which we live. "You shall be free indeed," writes Kahlil Gibran, "not when your days are without a care nor your nights without a want and a grief, but rather when these things girdle your life and yet you rise above them naked and unbound." If we never know suffering then our inner gospel peace will lie as fallow as a field that has never yielded to the plough. All Christian suffering is the seed of peace which must be planted deep within our souls so that its branches may reach out like a cross to every part of our lives. The growing process will disturb and stretch us and eventually bring us peace.

3

Being Prepared To Be Poor

Detachment

Poverty like suffering is an essential gospel word. Essential in the sense that if we take poverty out of the Christian Gospel then we will fail utterly to understand the Gospel, or the true meaning of the life style of Jesus. Poverty is the key which unlocks the mystery of his life and peace. "Sell what you own," said Jesus to the rich young man, "give the money to the poor, then come follow me" (Matthew 19:21). I look at my car, my fairly comfortable way of life, and I find this statement most disturbing. Is it really necessary to be so drastic about my worldly possessions if I want to be a Christian? What does Jesus mean by poverty? Isn't this saying of his inclined to be too dramatic in order to stress the importance of working for the coming of God's kingdom on earth? Do I have to take it literally? Do I have to be poor in order to experience gospel peace? Can't I be comfortable in my possessions and still be a Christian? And yet I have more than a sneaking feeling that I am cheating on the gospel message of poverty, and missing out on the deeper meaning of gospel peace. I have been peaceful in my life – known peace at its deepest – only when I have turned to God in complete trust. Does money prevent this attitude of total dependence on God?

In common with other Christians I know only too well that Jesus said: "You cannot be the slave of God and money" (Matthew 6:24). Here for "money", as we will see later, we can substitute anything which is not God's will for us, whether it be a wrong relationship, or a way of life in which we know we are not living as Jesus would in our own particular set of circumstances. Jesus saw "money" as a danger, a drug on which we would become too dependent. Eventually this dependence on "money" dilutes our dependence on God our Father to provide us with all that we need both spiritually and temporally. If I want to grow in gospel peace then I have to get my attitude to God right, and adjust accordingly the way I live my life. The coinage I must value is stamped with the seal of total obedience to God my Father. This is pure gold. The advice of Jesus is clear for those who want his peace. "Do not store up treasures for yourself on earth, where moths and woodworms destroy them and thieves can break in and steal. But store up treasures for yourselves in heaven, where neither moth nor woodworms destroy them and thieves cannot break in and steal. For where your treasure is, there will your heart be also" (Matthew 6:19–21).

The world claims that "money" brings the peace of security and that this is true peace, but Jesus holds the opposite viewpoint. Let us look at Matthew's text again about God and "money": "No one can be the slave of two masters: he will either hate the first and love the second or treat the first with respect and the second with scorn. You cannot be the slave of God and 'money' " (6:24). In order to understand the text I turn to Jesus so that from his life style I can judge what he thought of "money". His answer is unambiguous. In his own life style he saw material poverty as a means to his inner peace, because through it he expressed his total dependence on God his Father. It is to this challenge of gospel poverty, which brings deep inner peace, that as a Christian I have to respond in my own way. At first glance Jesus seems to be asking too much of me if I want peace, and yet his life style is the yardstick of mine.

41

He saw that he himself and his disciples could not be materially rich and preach in all its *fullness* his Gospel of trusting God completely with everything in life. But that was two thousand years ago, and right at the beginning of the Church. Can't I live a more diluted form of poverty in my twentieth-century world and still be a full Christian? Jesus distrusted money because he believed that it often robs us of our need to trust in God's providence, and in this respect it is as dangerous to the soul as drugs, drink and smoking are to the body. It is evil because it comes between us and God. So to get to grips with the problem of wealth I have to look more closely at the life of Jesus. Perhaps we know how Jesus lived because we have read it so many times, but repetition may have dulled the message. Let us look at it again under the aspect of poverty.

Poverty and peace were synonymous to Jesus because he wanted his life style to be seen as a sign of contradiction to the world. He deliberately chose actual poverty at the age of thirty when most men in their search for happiness would have opted for security and privilege. He was the *anauwin*, the poor man of the Bible, and he is to poverty what Mahatma Gandhi is to non-violence. He was born in a stable which, like his grave, belonged to another so that from start to finish his life could be reckoned among the most despised and the poorest of men. He borrowed a donkey for his royal entry into Jerusalem, and an upper room in which to celebrate his unique passover meal which is, and will be, the source of spiritual wealth for all his followers to the end of time. He left his home, his friends and his mother behind him to be free, as the Holy One of Israel, to preach his Gospel of healing and forgiveness. "Foxes have holes and the birds of the air have nests, but the Son of Man has nowhere to lay his head" (Matthew 8:20).

He was a friend to everyone, rich and poor alike, but he was only too well aware of the danger of riches, against which he warned his hearers time and again. "But alas for you who are rich; you are having your consolation now. Alas for you who have your fill now; you shall go hungry. Alas for you who laugh now; you shall mourn and weep" (Luke 6:24–25). He had little time for worldly power, and so while he did not have anything to say before the powerful Sanhedrin who tried him for his life, or before the pompous Herod who wanted to use him as a jester, nevertheless he spoke eloquently and compassionately to the crowds of ordinary, simple people who were hungry for a meaning to life. His preaching of total, selfless love of his Father, which had crowds flocking to every town and village he entered, attracted thousands into the desert much as did the Pied Piper of Hamelin. Yet in the end his popularity seemed to go sour and his own people, many of whom had seen his miracles and benefited from them, harassed their Roman overlord for his death as a criminal and blasphemer. They preferred a brigand to the man who spoke about an elusive kingdom which was not of this world. Because their values were wrong they wanted a wealthy kingdom here and now.

One of his closest friends sold him for a handful of silver, and picked him out as in an identity parade, and the rest of his followers ran away or denied him in his moment of crisis. The pagan soldiers valued his seamless robe more than they did his body; they did not want to tear his robe, and so played dice for it, while they lacerated his body with lashes, a crown of thorns, nails and a spear. That was how much they valued the Nazarene and his way of life with his Gospel of Peace, which for three short years in their military province had stood the world's standards on its head.

He was crucified in the shame of nakedness between two thieves, and as he lay dying he prayed for his enemies, "Father, forgive them"; he made a promise to a thief; gave his Mother to a young boy and his spirit to his Father. Thus ended a life so full of promise, so empty of achievement by worldly standards, a life of peace which ended with violence. Yet two days later he walked in the morning air and spoke again: "Peace be with you." We know that within his life and his message of peace there is enshrined his gospel of poverty, and surrender to his Father's will in everything, which will disturb the conscience of his followers as long as anyone will dare to call himself a Christian. If Jesus needed to be actually poor what right have we to want to be materially rich and still expect to find peace of soul?

Such in brief outline is the man of poverty and peace who came that we might have life to the full in his peace. It is difficult at times to see the connection between Christian poverty as Jesus lived it and peace of soul, yet for Jesus they are interchangeable realities; I cannot have one without the other. Poverty, like peace, is a word full of mystery and apparent contradictions. The reason why I am not at peace within myself is basically due to the fact that I have not come to terms with my life in the world, with the special kind of gospel poverty which Jesus demands of me if I am to follow him. He was at peace because he surrendered his whole life to God. If I am to be really rich in his peace then I must be prepared, when he calls me, to become poor for his sake. This means, quite simply, among other things, that whenever the level of my worldly wealth rises like a flood and threatens to drown my inner sense of values, my "Christian self", then I have to reduce my hold on wealth until such time as it subsides and once again comes under the control of the gospel message which means surrender of my whole life to God as a loving Father. The world with its glorification of wealth and power can so possess us that it unbalances our Christian peace, draws us away from the life style of Jesus, and dries up our love of God our Father. We become dependent on it rather than on God and so get our priorities wrong.

Excessive dependence on material security is dangerous for a Christian and is a drug I cannot afford to tamper with once I really love God, who ultimately provides for me as a Father. When I surrender my life to him, then money will lose its unreal importance and hold over me. After all, I am only a pilgrim in this village which we call earth. This is the attitude I should have if I want to become "poor in spirit" and rich in God's love as the gospel would have me be. If I love God then I should be prepared, if the Gospel demands it in my situation, to let go of everything, friends, home, my accustomed way of life, because that is the way he wants me to follow his Son. But is this what he really wants from me? –because as far as material possessions are concerned, while I am not obsessed by them, nevertheless I do not find poverty attractive even from a spiritual point of view. If I were set down in the middle of the squalor of the Third World I don't think I would be very happy, or say my prayers particularly well; in fact such poverty would distract me. It is a way of life I have never known and find difficult to imagine. But *if* it happened then I know God would equip me for my new life.

When I meditate prayerfully on his words I believe Jesus' Gospel is telling me not to get a thing about wealth, whether the accumulation or the lack of it. It does not matter whether I am rich or poor. All I have to do is to concentrate on the one thing necessary in life, namely, the love and service of God my Father. When the time comes for me to make sacrifices he will let me know and give me the grace to let go. If I surrender to him in little things day by day at the end I shall surrender my life itself. It is all part of the process of growing in gospel peace. Poverty is linked to my hold on this world and on my life itself. The truly poor man is not afraid to die.

St Paul puts the world and its false materialistic values into proper perspective when he relates it to his desire to love and follow Christ. "I believe nothing can happen that will outweigh the supreme advantage of knowing Christ Jesus my Lord. For him I have accepted the loss of everything, and I look on everything as so much rubbish if only I can have Christ and be given a place in him" (Philippians 3:8). I have to get my priorities right; nothing compares with my total attachment to Christ. The rich look at their riches in the world's eyes; the poor in spirit, who are prepared to lose everything, look at their poverty in Christ's. I may be afraid to change my life style and follow Christ, yet if I fail to answer his call then my life will become empty. Is it not a fact that many church-going people are not at peace in their souls because the gospel teaching of Christ on poverty has never come alive for them or made demands on their comfortable, secure lives? Respectability carried to excess is unacceptable to the true Christian. There is too much of it in our churches which too often have become glorified social clubs with "perks" for their members. Isn't this why the Jews are often seen, quite wrongly, as sharing a mutual assistance society rather than a faith in their God who brought them out of slavery into the Promised Land?

When I apply the teaching of Jesus on God and money to my own situation then I find that Christian poverty, like gospel peace, disturbs my way of life. It reveals to me in a startling way the true meaning of a life of inner peace and Christian fulfilment. If I want nothing from the world I can never be disappointed. This Gospel, if I am prepared to live it out, will lead me along strange and mysterious ways where material security or power are concerned. The world is not the master of my life, and neither am I the master of my own destiny. Because I have dared to put God first in my life I cannot guarantee what will happen tomorrow in my life if I am prepared to be at his beck and call. I cannot make plans for tomorrow because he has called me one day at a time. This is the essence of the Gospel, and the correct attitude of the Christian pilgrim.

Jesus' invitation to me to "Come, follow me" is at once a challenge and a threat to my way of life and inner peace. Like Peter, I want to know what the consequences involved in such a commitment are: "What about us?", he asked him, "we have left everything and followed you." Jesus said, "I tell you solemnly, there is no one who has left house, brothers, sisters, mother, father, children or land for my sake and for the sake of the Gospel who will not be repaid a hundred times over, houses, brothers, sisters, mother, children and land – not without persecutions – now in this present time, and in the world to come, eternal life" (Mark 10:28–30). I have the Lord's promise so why am I still worried, not only about my security and future, but my inner peace? The answer is simple. I just have not got enough faith and trust in the love and power of the Lord to fulfil his promise to me. I want the parachute of security to break my fall when I let go of wealth. I want to be at peace but in fairly comfortable, congenial surroundings. And yet if I am not poor enough in spirit within myself to trust him with my life then how can I honestly say that I am a full Christian in search of gospel peace? If I am brutally frank with myself then I must admit that I do not really value what a precious gift he offers me when he calls me to imitate his life of poverty. I want my pound of flesh now, and in this I am in "good" company with my fellow Christians of the Western world.

Poverty of spirit leads to love. Perhaps the reason there is not sufficient love in our churches is because we seem to be very lenient and ambiguous when we start explaining what Jesus meant by poverty. This, I most strongly believe, is due to a bad conscience on our part in the West. Jesus' teaching on poverty in his Sermon on the Mount is quite clear; he puts it at the top of his list of Beatitudes. While the accounts of his sermon differ – "How happy are you who are poor" (Luke 6:20); "How happy are the poor in spirit" (Matthew 5:3) – nevertheless gospel poverty is necessary to enter the kingdom of heaven in so far as we cannot be attached to the world and all that this involves, especially money, and be a real Christian. We cannot whittle away poverty in spirit until it means nothing. Poverty of spirit means *total* dependence on God. This poverty of spirit is as necessary for the poor as well as for the rich, because if the poor covet the riches of others in order to become rich themselves this too is unChristian, because it means that they are not happy with their lot in life. Detachment from worry about material goods sets us free to love God.

Money is one of the things that can erode our poverty of spirit if it takes us away from living out the full meaning of the Gospel of total dependence on God. If we are poor and are constantly preoccupied with the problem of how to become rich, or if we are wealthy and are greedy to make even more money, then our Christian priorities have been allowed to get out of focus. There is no doubt whatsoever that both Matthew and Luke see a necessary connection between some form of actual poverty and holiness. What form this actual poverty takes depends on each individual's conscience. If as a Christian I happen to be so materially rich that I become preoccupied with my wealth, then I have an added obstacle to overcome because I shall then need to cultivate a detached attitude to my possessions of which I am only the steward, in order to live the Christian life. Money is the alluring siren which entices us onto the rocks which destroy our sense of spiritual values. I also believe that every Christian should condemn as evil that type of poverty which means living in subhuman conditions, not only because of what such poverty does to its victims, but also because it is ultimately caused by the greed of those who have too much. We all know that the Third World exists because of the sinful greed of others. Money, like drink, is good when it is taken in due moderation.

The Gospel so highlights the actual poverty of Jesus that as a Christian I need to take another look, not only at my possessions, but at my whole life style and my standard of values. The test which poverty puts to us is this: What things am I prepared to give up if and when the Lord asks? The love of God is the essential element of poverty of spirit as taught and lived by Jesus. Without it poverty is meaningless. Being unencumbered with the world's goods leaves me free to love God, and this is its only purpose. *The only wealth in poverty is that it helps us to become rich in God's love.* St Paul puts his finger on the true purpose of poverty: "If I give away all that I possess, piece by piece, and if I even let them take away my body to burn it, but am without love, it will do me no good whatever" (1 Corinthians 13:3). The widow's mite in the gospel story will always remain relatively precious because of its value through generous love in real giving and sharing. "This poor widow has put more in than all who have contributed to the treasury; for they have all put in money they had over, but she from the little she had to live" (Mark 12:43–44).

There is little encouragement for the Christian in our consumer society to understand the meaning of gospel poverty. The churches, as I wrote earlier in this chapter, have played down the Gospel of actual poverty in the West because lurking at the back of our minds there is a haunting suspicion that our own life style is not as detached as it should be. We don't want to frighten our congregations away by emphasizing poverty. We may give money for charitable causes to ease our consciences or, worse still, to make us feel good, but it is comparatively easy to give from our plenty rather than our poverty. We can give and still remain materially rich because we have never experienced real poverty. It is the love with which we give that really enriches the gift. Kahlil Gibran reminds us: "There are those who have little and give it all. These are the believers in life and the bounty of life, and their coffer is never empty."

Just as the excess of drugs or drink can affect our bodies and minds adversely, so also over-attachment to money can destroy not only our spiritual lives, but ourselves and our families as well. "Frank" is a typical example of what I mean. When I first knew him twenty years ago he was a happily married man with a loving wife and a lovely young daughter. His wife helped him in every way to succeed in his business but her main priority was her home. Frank had within him a restlessness to succeed which was a compensation for the fact that his own parents were poor and not very loving, and so he always needed to prove something to himself. He spent longer hours away from home looking after his expanding business, and in the process drifted away from his wife and daughter. He bought them a colossal mansion as proof to himself, as much as to them, how well he was providing for them.

The end of the story is sad. His daughter's life is in a mess and she has rejected her father completely as well as the society which made him so. She has been in trouble with the police several times. His wife divorced him and is now living very happily with her second husband in a simple but loving home. Frank is still going from strength to strength in his business, has a new young "shallow" wife and often talks about his "ungrateful" family. But there are times, especially when he has had too much alcohol – which happens with greater frequency – when he confides in me. Then he vacillates between anger and sadness at the break-up of his marriage. Inner peace is something he has never experienced. He has damaged many people by his false set of values, not least of all himself. His search for "happiness" destroyed the real happiness of those he claimed to love. Frank, was, I believe, basically greedy and selfish even though he would thoroughly disagree with this assessment of his attitude. He would soon point out to me all he had materially given to his wife and daughter, yet he forgot to give his love which it was their right to expect.

In a sense Frank broke the First Commandment when he allowed money to become his god. "Michael", however, is a case of someone who came to grips with the money problem, and found a Christian solution for himself and his family. He was a successful lawyer, but as he said himself, "It was a terrible life. I was working sometimes from four in the morning until eight at night to make money I did not need. At the weekend there would be as many as sixty phone calls. I never saw the children. Financially I cannot afford to leave the practice, but spiritually I cannot afford to stay." He also had doubts about the morality of his profession in which he said, "conveyancing is a fraud on the public". He sold up his suburban home and moved to a farm with his wife and their twelve children. He thinks the decision was the right one for his family and himself because he believes that the opposite would be "immoral, weak, cowardly and selfish".

Jesus' teaching on poverty is not an easy one. It will make me ask questions about my life style and I cannot see myself coming up with an easy answer. And yet until I adjust my attitude to money I will never experience gospel peace. I know that if I were to live for myself alone and get a thing about my security, especially in my old age, then eventually I have only myself to live with. Fear of losing out, of not keeping up materially with the others, which might make me do strange things in the prime of life in order to succeed and be accepted socially, will come back to haunt me with their shadows and whispers in the autumn of my life, when the still small voice of conscience is heard again, and justice draws back the veil on my selfish past. Jesus reminds me time and again through his life style that his peace "is not of this world". Like love, it cannot be bought.

Money for Jesus is but the tip of the iceberg. My reaction to it is the barometer of my spiritual life. Of course there are more important things to life than money, and there are many rich people who give their time and talents to the service of the Lord. Yet the warning about "money" and the privilege it brings is very clear in the Gospel. Once I really want to grow in poverty of spirit then I shall be prepared "to be least and last" as well as living my life "one day at a time". They are the twin guidelines along which my Christian life must run if its destination is true gospel peace. As I develop in my Christian life then I shall become more single-minded of purpose and seek the one thing necessary for salvation. The coinage of my life will bear the stamp of God and not that of Caesar. Simplicity will be the keynote of my life, which I shall live from day to day without worry or anxiety. With Christ at my side I have all the wealth I need in this life and the next. This is the source of my peace and my spiritual wealth.

4

Being Prepared To Be Least and Last

Simplicity

Most of us say unthinkingly that we love the simple life. But is this true? If it were we would all be committed Christians, because the life of Jesus could be summed up in one word – simplicity. Like his peace he offers us his simplicity. His simple approach to everything in life gave him insights unique to any spiritual leader. The secret of his simplicity and peace was that he was at one with his Father's will, and this was the driving force which motivated him. The advice Jesus gives to me, and to all who seek his peace and want to be like him, is this: "Set your hearts on God's kingdom first, and on his righteousness, and all these other things will be given you as well" (Matthew 6:33). He tells me that once I put my values in life in their proper perspective then I shall experience his peace, which is not of this materialistic world but of the Kingdom of God. My life will be shot through with the presence and righteousness of God once I seek him in everything. But how does one become so single-minded of purpose, and what does it involve? Is it easy to be simple in our complex consumer society? What does Jesus mean by simplicity? Simplicity seems a straightforward word but like peace, suffering and poverty it takes a lifetime to plumb the depths of its meaning. It is an essential gospel word.

If gospel poverty is difficult for me then so is simplicity, which is just another way of looking at it. If I practise one then the other follows automatically. Jesus said in the Sermon on the Mount that his Father's Kingdom belongs only to the "poor in spirit". "How happy are the poor in spirit," he said, "theirs is the kingdom of heaven" (Matthew 5:3). For Jesus the "poor in spirit" are the "least and the last" in a greedy world conscious of so-called greatness and power which place one person above another. Poverty of spirit is, in fact, for Jesus a paradox. It is to be poor as far as the world is concerned but to be really rich in the things of the spirit. Simplicity, like poverty, turns the world's standards upside down. It is to rate God's will as supreme and to put the world's value at zero. It is, in other words, to be high on the kingdom of God and low on the kingdom of the world. I achieve this by seeking and doing God's will in everything in my life.

The peaceful person is poor in spirit and is prepared to be "least and last". It is this simplicity of attitude in just wanting to do God's will which makes me prepared as a Christian to be "least and last" in the world's eyes, and thus the "greatest and first" in the Kingdom of God. Riches, power and privilege should have no hold over me because in Jesus I have overcome the world. The spirit I should follow belongs to the Kingdom of God and not to the world. This is the kingdom that as a Christian I choose to seek. When I am "least and last" in the spirit of the world I become one of God's children depending on him for the things that really matter for what I want to do with my life. Because I seek God's kingdom first and his righteousness, the rest of my life falls into line. Once I stray away from this objective then life becomes complicated. I shall find myself in all sorts of compromise with my Christian faith, when I lose my grip on the "one thing necessary" which will always remain the Kingdom of God. Everything else is evaluated from that. It is the yardstick of my life which is lived in the light of the Gospel. I know from experience how many times I have compromised my Christian vocation because I allowed the world to get a grip on me. Life as a Christian became at these times both complicated and pharisaical.

"Poverty of spirit" for Jesus goes hand in hand with the "spiritual childhood" or "humility" which is required for entry into God's kingdom. In this *humility* lies the measure of the greatness of a Christian. The Kingdom of God is the only thing of true value and is the rare treasure through which, if I really want it and find it, I shall become truly rich. Jesus constantly stressed the unique value of God's kingdom and his righteousness, before which everything in our world pales into insignificance. "The Kingdom of Heaven is like a merchant looking for rare pearls; and when he finds one of great value he goes and sells everything he owns and buys it" (Matthew 13:44–46). Those who are humble may seem to be "least and last" but are in point of fact the "greatest and the first", because they possess the pearl of great price. And all this because *the world has got a completely wrong notion of what true greatness is.*

Jesus is the way to union with the Father. He is the signpost we must follow in order to arrive at our destination. He commands us to "set your hearts on God's kingdom first and on his righteousness" (Matthew 6:34). The world has false status symbols, which are road signs placed by the Devil to point out the wrong direction. Jesus himself was tempted in the desert to bow down as the Devil put before him the false attractions of this world: "Next, taking him to a very high mountain, the Devil showed him all the kingdoms of the world and their splendour. 'I will give you all these,' he said, 'if you fall at my feet and worship me.' Then Jesus replied, 'Be off, Satan! For scripture says: You must worship the Lord your God, and serve him alone' "(Matthew 4:8–10). The world's false values will always have an attraction for our "selfish selves", but its pleasures never make for true gospel peace which alone comes from loving service of God who always comes first in our lives. If we serve the world then we have our reward already. If we compromise as Christians then our lives lose the savour of the Gospel. The directness of the Gospel message is lost.

"You serve God," says Jesus, "in simplicity." When I reflect on my life and work things out for myself, then I acknowledge that it is always the simple things in life that bring me real peace. The memories of the joys of my youth are always centred on the simple things which gave me great enjoyment and never cost a penny. The most generous Christians I ever met in my life were those in the two poor parishes I served in the early years of my priesthood. They were a real family in the Christian sense of the word, with whom I had deep, meaningful relationships. I experienced more love and peace among them than I did from subsequent sophisticated, well-heeled congregations. The poor were aware of God in their lives and wanted to serve him as best they could. The secret of their holiness was their directness and simplicity. It is the same with my Christian life. If all I want is to serve God then my life has a directness and honesty about it, a simplicity, which is in sharp contrast to the world's guile and duplicity. I remember with a sense of shame hearing someone in a very high position in the Church priding himself on being an ecclesiastical Kissinger.

True greatness for Jesus means that we must remain children of the Kingdom, which does not mean that we are not to think for ourselves, but rather that we are to grow spiritually through an increasing awareness of God's love for us as Father. The older we get, and the more Christian we become, the greater will be our appreciation of the mysteries of our faith. We do not grow in faith through flights of speculative theological fantasy. Simplicity takes us into the heart of the mysteries of the Kingdom. Christmas will be as fresh for us as when we came as toddlers to the crib, and Easter will renew us with new hope and life just as vigorously as the day when we first realized that Jesus did in fact rise from the dead. Being a Christian makes me for ever young, as each day in life fills me with surprises and challenges. I look on the world with wonder, not cynicism. Money can never buy this zest for living to the full which is our birthright as Christians. The simple Christian is for ever grateful for small mercies, and gratitude is the best form of response to God, who is seen as a loving Father who never forgets us.

Simplicity is a precious gift for every age in my life; it is for the young, the middle-aged and the old. Because it is very precious it can easily be lost or blunted. When the apostles argued among themselves as to who was the greatest Jesus was ready with his answer: "He took a little child and set him by his side and said to them, 'Anyone who welcomes this little child in my name welcomes me; and anyone who welcomes me welcomes the one who sent me. For the least among you all, that is the one who is great'" (Luke 9:46–48). As long as I avoid falling into the trap of becoming one of the world's sophisticates I shall remain one of God's children, and it is to the little ones, the humble, that the mysteries of God's kingdom are revealed. This spiritual childhood is as necessary to us as baptism, since it is in this simplicity or poverty of spirit that we grow as Christians in our understanding of the Christian faith. "I bless you, Father, Lord of heaven and earth, for hiding these things from the learned and clever, and revealing them to mere children!" (Luke 10:21).

"Be a child of the kingdom," says Jesus, "and you will soon discover what loving service of God really means." Children who remain unspoilt and live in the rough and tumble of a family, serve about the house in order to help their parents. They do not think any task too menial for them because they are doing it for the ones they love. In his philosophy of "least and last" Jesus gives me the example of service in his own life which flows from his poverty and simplicity. He tells me that I am not to consider myself superior to anyone else, but to regard myself as a servant, since in his eyes we are all brothers and sisters in this world. If there is any distinction to be made then it is the poor ones who are to be preferred because they are lowly in the world's estimation and are generally treated unjustly. Jesus told the followers of John the Baptist that they were to report back to their leader and tell him of all they had seen: "the dead are raised to life and the Good News is proclaimed to the poor" (Matthew 11:5). In other words, making the Gospel come alive for the underprivileged and rejects of society is as important as raising the dead to life. In both the saving power of the Resurrection is at work.

Because he is humble Jesus is the model servant of God. At the Last Supper, when he washed the feet of his disciples, and served them at table, he gave them explicit instructions as to their attitude towards each other: "The greatest among you must behave as if he were the youngest, the leader as if he were the one who serves. For who is the greater, the one at table or the one who serves? The one at the table, surely? Yet here I am among you as one who serves" (Luke 22:26–27). The servant is like the child, "least and last", who serves the Christ in others because of the Christ within himself. Like Christ we are to be humble and not claim privilege because Christ himself was humble and "did not cling to his equality with God but emptied himself to assume the condition of a slave" (Philippians 2:6–7).

But is this the case with us today? Are we Christians regarded as the humble servants of man's needs, or are we, by and large, indistinguishable from those who live by the world's standards? There is little cause for satisfaction on

our part in the West when we look at Jesus' gospel of
simplicity, because we have all strayed very far from the
gospel ideal of humble service, of being "least and last".
The reason for our failure is obvious. We have imitated the
world's concept of power in our churches and personal
lives, which is alien to the thinking and practice of Jesus
and the Early Church. Jesus gave the world a new type of
humble leadership which was totally encompassed by
service of others in all that he was and had. He told his
apostles: "You know that among the pagans the rulers lord
it over them, and their great men make their authority felt.
This is not to happen among you. No, anyone who wants
to be *great* among you must be your servant, and anyone
who wants to be *first* among you must be your slave, just as
the Son of Man came not to be served but to serve, and to
give his life as a ransom for many" (Matthew 20:25–28).
The paradox of simplicity is essential to the Gospel of
Jesus. Efficient institutions find it hard to understand and
imitate. They are, in fact, pagan by Jesus' standards, in so
far as they do not find the same need to trust God because
they are so efficient. Efficiency breeds self-sufficiency and
excludes God from his rightful place in our lives.

True, we must work as if everything depended on us, and
have a pride in what God allows us to do for the spread of
his Kingdom, but we have to be on our guard against false
spiritual pride and self-righteousness. Pride and
triumphalism have no part in Jesus' make-up. By his simple
servant's life Jesus exorcised Christians for ever of all false
secular power and of worldly privilege and preferment. In
his teaching he said, "Beware of the scribes who like to
walk about in long robes, to be greeted obsequiously in the
market squares, to take the front seats in the synagogues
and the places of honour at banquets; these are the men
who swallow the property of widows, while making a
show of lengthy prayers. The more severe will be the

sentence they receive" (Mark 12:38–40). The only power Jesus exercised in his Father's name was over sin, disease and evil spirits. It was the rabbinical power of the Jews which ultimately betrayed him into the hands of his enemies. Great people in the world's eyes will find little comfort in his gospel of service. His followers were to be the servants of all, and the service of their lives through humility was their witness in their world to God as the loving Father of everyone. It was his will which they were constantly to seek and obey whatever the cost to themselves. Like Jesus it was what pleased the Father which was the motivating influence in their lives. This down the centuries would often cause them to seek the "least and last" positions in their social spheres, and so the religious vocation of poverty was born. The Pope has as one of his titles "Servant of the servants", and this is what I and every Christian should aim to be. The church today that really humbles itself to become the servant of all is proving itself to be Christ's Church in the world.

But I see power and privilege at work on all sides, even in the churches, so how can I react in a positive and Christian way? I have, of course, to reject it in my own life and not to condone it in others. The only way for me is to live my life as a Christian servant of the Gospel and pray that others will follow. Since being a servant does not confer rank then it is not something for which the worldly have a burning ambition. If equality for all frightens the privileged – and what a sad thing that privilege plays such a large part in the bureaucracy of the Christian churches – then what must happen to them when the word "servant" is mentioned? Is not this exactly the word Jesus used time and again to describe his followers? His kingdom, he repeatedly stressed, was not of this world or its power structures which enslave people, preventing them from growing as children of his Father. The pharisees were wrong, said

Jesus, because "they tie up heavy burdens and lay them on men's shoulders" (Matthew 23:5). Worldly people feel secure by having others under their control. Jesus warns us of the evils of those goods or rank which might put us in a superior position of privilege over another. I must be poor in gospel terms or I shall fail to remember that all goods, and positions of power, are subordinate to the person; "surely life means more than food, and the body more than clothing" (Matthew 6:25). When I think of the needs and rights of others I soon forget "my selfish self" and my false notions of self-importance. There is so much to be done in the service of the Gospel that I have no time to think of myself but only of him. The church, therefore, that forgets itself in the service of the gospel is the true Church of Christ. The Church of Christ is for mission and service, not preservation and privilege.

If all Christians followed the gospel of *service in simplicity* through to its logical conclusion, not only would there be peace in our hearts, but also between the churches. Sadly this is not so, and while claiming to be Christians it is we who, even in the name of the Gospel, erect barriers of distrust between peoples, cultures, religions and nations. Christian disunity is a scandal and is alien to the Gospel. If we look to Christ more, and to our institutional structures less, then the path to unity would be cleared of many obstacles which today seem insurmountable. "But now in Christ Jesus, you that used to be so far apart from us have been brought very close, by the blood of Christ. For he is the peace between us, and has made the two into one and broken down the barrier which used to keep them apart, actually destroying in his own person the hostility caused by the rules and decrees of the Law" (Ephesians 2:13–16). The Maranatha Community, composed of all the mainstream churches, see each other as Christians rather than as members of any denomination.

It is this Christian Gospel of the brotherhood of man and service rather than privilege which is mine today as a Christian once I dare to cast aside the cloak of superiority, and reject the world's values which divide people from each other. A child will innocently play with his neighbour whatever his colour, religion or social class, until his parents forbid him to do so. They project their prejudices onto him, which they in turn inherited from their parents. It is adults, with their false divisive standards, who not only make wars, but segregate their children into factions which erupt into social or even religious violence. The sins of the parents are being visited on their children. Isn't Northern Ireland a typical example? I remember a few years ago playing with a child in Belfast when the mother came out and scolded him for being friendly with a Papist. The next time I saw him I noticed hostility in the child's eyes. He was just four years old. We refuse to acknowledge that even though Jesus Christ is Lord of our lives he is also the Lord of the lives of those who do not belong to our religious denomination. We become an exclusive brethren and deep down in our souls we know that this is wrong. This exaggerated idea of our own exclusive hold on God's truth and grace disturbs our peace of soul because we know that this is not according to the mind of Jesus.

The individual is supremely important in Jesus' Gospel because when we are all "poor in spirit" as children of the Kingdom then no one is superior to another. We are all God's children who are not rich in our own name but in our Father's. This is his gift to us. Christians, therefore, are not to regard themselves as superior to their pagan neighbours but are instead to be servants of the Gospel. This attitude of simplicity makes us humble servants of the Gospel. Too many Christians, unfortunately, are self-righteous and smug about the certainty of their own salvation. Self-righteousness, like power, corrupts us in the depths of our Christian personality, and destroys our gospel peace. If I am really prepared to be "last and least" then I do not really care who is above me on the worldly scale. Once I forget service and cultivate power then I am, of course, heading for spiritual destruction. Perhaps that is why institutional churches have been rejected so readily by our world searching for God, yet not finding him in ecclesiastical power structures. Is it not a fact that in every walk of life it is the exception who is not changed by fame and fortune, so that when the exception comes forward he is greeted with rapturous enthusiasm and love by people starved of seeing humble Christian service in high places?

Our Christian faith is a gift which puts us at the service of everyone. We have freely received and we must freely give without expecting any return: "You received without charge, give without charge" (Matthew 10:8). We will experience peace of soul through the knowledge that what we have received in our faith has been given by God without let or hindrance. If we are truly Christian then we will not block its flow to others through our narrowness of mind and heart. We will as Christians always seek God's righteousness without ever becoming self-righteous. We know that through God's grace we are part of his unique Church and Body. If we think, however, that because we are Christians we are therefore better than anyone else we will never know "kingdom peace", because in the process we will dilute our faith into a divisive religion rather than one of the service of the Gospel.

Lest I, too, become self-righteous even about those whom I think are self-righteous I have only to look at myself and my own selfishness to realize that I also have feet of clay. I remind myself constantly how dangerously self-destructive secular power and spiritual arrogance are, and I seek their presence in my Christian life as avidly as a poisonous snake. I have to be on my guard against flattery and all forms of self-deception because the wrong use of power damages people. It is this which disturbs the peace of the churches in their search for unity, because they too are unwilling to be "least and last" and are more interested often in defending their claims rather than seeking truth in mutual love, brotherhood and humility. This is my own experience. The power game does not end at the gates of a church.

Self-righteousness makes me think I am a better Christian because my church is better than any other Christian church. It also tends to make me look down on people who are not able to cope with the world, so that I regard them as "failures". This train of thinking is alien to that of Jesus who came into the world, as he said, "not to call the virtuous but sinners" (Mark 2:17). We priests deal with people who need help. If we were car dealers we would spend most of our time trying to get "old bangers" through their MOT rather than selling Rolls-Royces. A typical example of failure was "John" who, try as he might, was unable to conquer his craving for alcohol. He ruined his health, his wife and family left him, until eventually he was penniless having drunk himself out of a job and his home. I saw him at a very low ebb on many occasions and through his tears, not of self-pity but of an awareness of what he was doing to those he loved, I realized he had never lost his childlike trust in God. He was one of the most sincerely repentant persons I ever knew, and when I buried him there were few to mourn his passing.

In my heart I knew he was holy (great) in a most extraordinary way, and even though I do not condone his behaviour, I was privileged to be his friend. He hung on to God's love in all his difficulties, and now on reflection I continue to discover as time goes by more Christian qualities in him than in many other people whom the world and the churches regard as a success. Why he could not overcome his desire for drink is something I cannot answer except to quote again St Paul: "I cannot understand my own behaviour. I fail to carry out the things I want to do and I find myself doing the very things I hate" (Romans 7:15).

Since it is to such as John, "the least", that Jesus came with his gospel of forgiveness, then who am I to judge who is a success or failure in life? John, however damaging his weakness to himself and to others, always turned to God for forgiveness. His greatness lay in his childlike trust in God as a loving Father, even though he was bewildered by all the chaos he was causing in the lives of those who loved him. Many would condemn him as a moral failure, because the Pharisee still lives on in us. Our first inclination is to throw stones despite the fact that we live in spiritual glasshouses. Success in coping with life is judged by worldly standards which have crept into our moral judgements. We fail to be sufficiently self-critical, and it is to such as us that the Gospel speaks. "Why do you observe the splinter in your brother's eye," says Jesus, "and never notice the plank in your own?" (Matthew 7:3). Many of the moral failures in our world, whom sometimes we tend to regard as "least and last", may well be the "greatest and first" in the Kingdom of God for they are the poor for whom Jesus had a special love. When I become like a little child I can accept people for what they are in themselves, with all their weaknesses.

As long as I remain a child of the Kingdom, then to that extent, I am open at every turn in my life to God my Father. Whatever situation I may find myself in I hope I shall always seek his will. If it be his will that I am a success in the world's estimation of success, then I shall use my position to make his Kingdom come; if I seem to be a failure, I shall be equally happy because I have committed my life to him. The criterion of my true success or failure is that like a little child I trust him with my life and all I want to do is live for his Kingdom. It is this simplicity of "least and last" which ultimately disturbs me, at the same time as it brings me that deep peace of soul which nothing can destroy.

5

Living One Day At A Time

Trust

If Jesus wants us to live in peace then why doesn't he solve all our problems? Jesus is nothing if not honest. He knows that worry destroys peace. His philosophy of life is both simple and compassionate. I am to live, he said, one day at a time because "each day has enough troubles of its own" (Matthew 6:34). Each day has got problems with which I can cope, but these problems become worries and cause anxiety when I keep them from yesterday or even add on tomorrow's. The reason I am not to worry or be anxious about yesterday or tomorrow, is that worry takes my mind off the one thing necessary, namely, to love God my Father "now", at this moment of time, because I trust him with everything in my life. For Jesus a worried person is a divided person – not at peace – whatever the cause of his worry, because through worry he cannot live the present moment to the full. I cannot trust God if I worry unduly about my life and its problems. I have to face my problems like everyone else, but as a Christian I no longer face them alone. I take up my cross *daily* to follow him. He does not carry my cross, but the knowledge that he carried his for love of me helps me to carry mine.

If I fail to do as Jesus tells me, then by worrying I give myself too heavy a burden to carry, and thus the balance of my life and peace is disturbed. He reminds me that yesterday is dead and tomorrow is yet to come. He is the great teacher of the value of "now". Every day for the Christian is made up of moments of the "now" because life comes moment by moment. It is in living out each moment to the full that the balance of my Christian life is adjusted and maintained, and my peace preserved, even in the midst of the most shattering events. Jesus in every "now" is present to calm the troubled waters of my life. I always help the bereaved to take each day as it comes without their loved ones, rather than keep on repeating the slogan "Time is a great healer". To live one day at a time is as much as they can do.

I shall never be free from problems in my life but Jesus shows me how to deal with them. One of my favourite passages in the Gospel is recounted by Matthew shortly after the Sermon on the Mount. It is the perfect formula for peace for me as a Christian if I really want to grow in my trust of God throughout my life. "That is why I am telling you not to worry about your life and what you are to eat, nor about your body and how you are to clothe it. Surely life means more than food, and the body more than clothing. Can any of you, for all his worrying, add one single cubit to his span of life? So do not worry; do not say, 'What are we to eat? What are we to drink? How are we to be clothed?' It is the pagans who set their hearts on all these things. Your heavenly Father knows you need them all. Set your hearts on his kingdom first, and on his righteousness, and all these other things will be given you as well. So do not worry about tomorrow: tomorrow will take care of itself. Each day has enough trouble of its own" (Matthew 6:25–34).

In this text Jesus is not attacking money but *worry*. Jesus wants me to trust myself and every aspect of my life to God my Father, who knows all my needs including the material necessities which money can buy. He knows what is necessary for my peace. Love and trust of God as a Father, says Jesus, are far more important than money. What does it matter if I am materially poor as long as I set my heart on God's Kingdom? This trust in God as a Father who provides for us is a consequence of his teaching on poverty, and being prepared to be "least and last". Jesus asks me, therefore, not only to renounce the anxious pursuit of money as an insurance against future need, but any anxiety I may have about my present problem, whatever it be, for even this divides the heart. Anxiety and peace are incompatible. The anxious person is not a trustful person.

Is Jesus telling me then to lie back and leave everything to God? This sounds like a lazy way of opting out of my responsibility. Of course, says Jesus, we all have to work and plan – the word frightens me – for tomorrow, but eventually if I am a Christian then I must leave all the tomorrows of my life to God because it will take me all I can do to live out today to the full. As a Christian I have to get my problems into their right perspective or else I shall get a thing about them, and so begin to worry, especially about my security for tomorrow. The philosophy of Jesus is this: look around you and realize that if the Creator provides so well for creatures at a material level, how much more the Father for his children in the things they need which really matter. So do not worry. Be at peace.

Jesus shows me what should be the real values in my life. He tells me to *value life* – "surely life means more than food" – and its dignity given to me by my Creator and Father, and to *appreciate the spiritual values* – "set your hearts on his Kingdom first and on his righteousness" – which will help me to grow as a fully human, integrated, peace-filled person. I am worth more than many sparrows to God because he made me in his own image and redeemed me through his only Son. This is my real worth; sparrows are bought two for a penny, but I am redeemed by the precious blood of Jesus, my Saviour. Problems like sparrows do not merit my worry. A sparrow falls to the ground, an event bursts unexpectedly upon me which temporarily disrupts my life, but my heavenly Father knows about it, and all will be well if I trust him. I do not know the answer now but it will come one day. I am at peace today because events in my life which disturbed me were left to God, and the peace he brought is something I shall never be able to describe.

Though I should walk in the valley of darkness he is there with me because his Son has been there before me. What God has done for me in the past he will do again. Worry about the past or the future is a sure sign of my lack of trust in God as a loving Father, and in his power and readiness to look after and provide for me. If I take each day in trust, with all its difficulties, I shall be doing exactly what the Father wants of me, because in this way I commit each day from dawn to dusk in trust to him. My Christian life will have the authentic ring of peace about it when I use each day as the "now" to do the Father's will as fully as possible as he unfolds it before me moment by moment, one day at a time. I know that when I once trust him with each day and hour of my life then the most extraordinary things happen. I have myriad examples of this in my life so that I have come to expect "surprises" from God. Here is just one.

In my first parish I had been saving up for four months to go home to my family in Ireland shortly after Christmas, and had accumulated the princely sum of £30, which was quite a lot in the early 'fifties. A few days before Christmas a couple came to the door in great distress. The husband apparently was entrusted by the wife to put a certain amount of money each week into a "Christmas cheer" fund which would provide them with presents for the children and extra for the festive table. Instead he had lost the money on backing horses which were too polite to be first past the post! In short, the couple were broke. In my naïvety I still like to believe that they only came to me for advice, but when I thought of the children I gave them all the money I had. I visited them on Christmas Day and shall never forget the delight of the children as they played with their new toys.

The father never repaid me, even though I can still hear his promises ringing in my ears, and I suppose he is still gambling. The story does not end there. On Christmas night, when I was still torn between anguish over the lost holiday for which I had planned so long, and my exhilaration of spirit, a parishioner handed me a small envelope with the words "Spend it on yourself, Father". When I opened it later I found six crisp five pound notes inside with a little card saying "Happy Christmas".

The Lord said that *the measure we give is the measure we receive*, and I have found this to be so all through my life. If we are generous with others then he is generous with us. I had my holiday, helped to make a family happy, received a handsome gift from a parishioner and all because it was Christmas. Who would dare to say that he does not believe in a God of surprises? I believe that my real problem in life is myself, and my lack of trust in God. He knows what he is about when he sends people into my life with their problems, and I give all I have to help them.

Certainly I must plan, but when the future becomes the "now" I have to learn to change course, to modify my plans in the light of the new situation. When I listened to the call of the moment that Christmas I had to adapt to the new circumstances which had arisen. I was happy saving for my holiday, happy in giving my savings to a poor family, and happy in receiving from a generous parishioner. This was the precise order which God wanted, and each giving or receiving was a "now". If I had given my savings *after* I had received my gift then what would have been the value in *real* giving by me, or would I have been so happy with the family on Christmas Day, or with the unexpected gift? If we never really give of ourselves to others then we are never really ever able to receive from God or anyone else. Every Christian has received far more than he could ever give to others. Do I really live by this truth? Perhaps if I start today to be more open to others, and allow Christ's peace to disturb me, then I shall really trust God with my life.

God knows what he is about, and real peace of soul begins when I stop wanting to fight the reality of the present moment as if it should not exist, and start to accept it for what it is. If the doctor tells me I have terminal cancer then I commit the first judgement and prognosis to God. It is unproductive on my part to keep on asking "Why?" instead of getting on with the living through each situation presented to me, and seeing it as God's will for me at this particular moment. I have lived out my Christian story in more dramatic ways in later years when faced with really big problems. Wherever I have been without planning it myself, God has used me to help people whom I might otherwise never have met. God put me into situations in my life when he knew I trusted him, and through them my faith in his love increased. All the credit must go to him because I am only the instrument of his peace. My ministry of healing in his name always bears fruit when I go to those people to whom he directs me. If for his sake I involve myself with others he involves himself with me. When God sends people to me in situations especially not of my own choosing I must grasp that situation as impatiently as did Jesus in the garden. "Get up, let us go," he commands his apostles; the time for waiting is over, the hour has come.

Troubles come our way; we do not have to invite them into our lives. A death in the family, a lack of faithfulness in one we love, a separation in marriage, the loss of employment, a physical or mental sickness which changes our accustomed life pattern, and a thousand and one sad events take us into the desert of loneliness so that we are thrown off balance. We are tempted to worry because we do not visualize how we can cope with our problems, or see the road ahead. For a while we lose our grip on inner peace. These are the storms in life which test whether or not the house of self is built on the rock of faith and trust in God, or on the sand of "selfish self". When an unexpected problem disrupts the smooth flow of our lives our Christian faith is being examined. We are being tested. The quality of our peace will soon be seen for what it is. How often have I seen people who go to church week after week unable to cope with a situation which requires deep faith and trust in God.

If I *worry* or am anxious about how I can cope with my problems then I am relying on my own resources and not on God's. As a Christian I am never alone. God who put me in this situation can change it. In other words, today's situation with its problems will not be the same tomorrow, and when tomorrow comes God will be there to help me find an answer, because when tomorrow comes it ceases to be tomorrow. It becomes today in which God is with me every moment. Tomorrow I shall just have to look at how the situation will be *then* because that is the problem I shall have to cope with in the *here and now*. I trust the future to God my Father in love, just as I commit my past to his mercy.

A typical example of what I mean is found in the gospel story of the holy women, hurrying through the streets of Jerusalem that first Easter morning to finish anointing the body of Jesus. They had been saying to one another, "Who will roll the stone away for us from the entrance to the tomb?" But when they looked they could see that the stone, which was very big, had already been rolled back

(Mark 16:3–4). They had a problem setting out for the tomb, and they were right to discuss it because they knew that their weak feminine strength could not shift the boulder. It would be foolhardy for them to engage in wishful thinking – "Wouldn't it be great if someone shifted it" – because such escapist imagining would not solve the problem. But on their arrival the situation had changed so that what they came to do, namely to anoint a corpse, was no longer necessary.

In the "now" of the Sunday their new problem is different to Friday's, "you must go and tell his disciples and Peter. He is going before you to Galilee; it is there you will see him, just as he told you" (Mark 16:7). Telling the frightened disciples was their problem for Easter Day. Now that they no longer had to concern themselves with rolling boulders away, they had to face a bigger problem because of the disciples' disbelief. They still had to roll away boulders but of a different kind. They were encouraged to tell their extraordinary story through the experience they already had of the empty tomb. The lesson for me as a Christian is obvious. When I face small problems by trusting in the Lord and committing them to his Resurrection then I am equipped to deal with bigger ones if and when they occur. Even though problems often increase rather than disappear yet I grow in inner strength and confidence through coping with them one at a time. In this way my gospel peace grows in depth and quality so that as problems grow so does my peace.

I used to worry needlessly, too, about things which never turned out as I feared. Imaginary worries can so plague our lives that we are unable to be at peace within ourselves, or have a good night's sleep which will prepare us for the morrow. How many times have we all worried about situations, which in fact never existed except in the dark corners of our imagination where the Devil

(Hinderer) does his best to disturb our peace of soul? I keep on saying to myself, "I can handle today's problems with God's help; tomorrow I shall leave everything to his providence too because he alone can change situations." An old lady, whenever she meets me, says "Not to worry", and she is right. We have to be honest with ourselves; our problems may be real, our worries are not.

Once I trust God with my life I shall soon discover that he has a delicious sense of humour. If I take my problems and myself too seriously there is something really missing in my life as a Christian. If I trust God as my Father then I shall soon discover that he has a wonderful facility for getting me out of embarrassing situations. What his Son did in Cana of Galilee to save the young couple faced with the problem of a lack of wine for their guests he does for us each day if only we knew it.

Here is another example from my own life. When the Wood Hall Centre at Wetherby in Yorkshire was first opened we were not as organized on the staff as we might have been. One Sunday afternoon three coach-loads of old people turned up to look around the place. We were tired after a heavy weekend conference, and were shattered when the trip organizers told us that they had ordered high tea. We had no record of such a request on our files, and there was literally nothing in the larder. Sister Jarlath, our cook, threw her hands up in despair and said to me: "This is too much. I suppose you expect God to come down and get a high tea for a hundred and fifty people." I laughed, but it was rather hollow as I shepherded our visitors to the chapel for an unscheduled Mass, where, tongue in cheek, I asked them to pray for a minor miracle. Ironically, the Gospel for the Sunday was the feeding of the five thousand in the desert, which I thought was rubbing liturgical salt into an open wound.

When we came back to the Centre there before my

astonished eyes was a magnificent meal of cooked hams, cakes of every variety, jellies and fruit. I had previously thought the cook was superb but this was miraculous! "Where did you get all the food from in such record time, with all the shops shut?" I asked her. She told me the story. Just *after* I had started Mass the Little Sisters of the Poor came in their van with the left-overs from their garden fête held the previous day. They thought we might be able to make use of the food, and they did not want to see it going to waste. How right they were! "Who told you we needed it?" I asked them. They replied, "No one. We just thought we would bring it." These Little Sisters do wonderful work looking after old people, and it was to old people that the meal was in fact given. The bewildered Sister Jarlath, with a twinkle in her eye, said: "I have seen everything now. I will never doubt again!" Who said God has no sense of humour? God runs the best catering service in the world because his shop is open twenty-four hours a day, seven days a week, and his only price is trust in his providence.

The lesson to be learned from the story is this: if God fed thousands in the desert is it likely that he will fail us over such a small thing as a high tea? As I was reading the Gospel at Mass, wondering what on earth was going to happen, the Little Sisters of the Poor were already at the Centre getting the meal ready. What God has done in the past he will do again, and is in fact doing now if only we had eyes of faith to see it. We *see* in time, God *acts* from eternity.

So many events like "the high tea affair" have happened in my life that more and more I trust God with my future and my past, because as a Christian I hope I am one of "today's people". I am not one of "yesterday's" or "tomorrow's people" because the spiritual "now" of today is the spiritual mercury of my life gauging my spiritual temperature, the compass which helps me to keep my life on course. When I live a life of faith and trust in God as a Father then this helps me to think positively and creatively through every "now" and its problems. This rids me of worry which destroys my peace of soul. Tomorrow's and yesterday's people are never at peace because they want to change the past, and bring the future under their sole personal control. Today's people see their lives as an ongoing, living partnership with God. It is a joint effort which brings peace.

Tomorrow's people do not know how to live: the widow, for example, who cannot face the future without the presence of her husband; the man who loses his job which means everything to him and is haunted by the fear of empty and meaningless days ahead; the arthritic who cannot put the dread out of her mind that one day her physical movements will be severely hampered and life will come to a standstill; the businessman who saves his money to provide for his retirement which he will probably never have. Their "todays" are lost by anticipating their "tomorrows".

How does all this come about? "Tomorrow's people" start their false and unChristian way of thinking at a very early age because for them the grass is greener on the other side of the fence. When they are young they imagine that it will be wonderful when they grow up and leave school to earn a living of their own and become independent. They enjoy their freedom only for a short while before they rush into marriage, where the honeymoon period does not usually last very long. So they look forward to having a family, and once that happens they cannot wait to get the children off to school so that they can have some free time of their own!

When the children grow up and marry they start turning the clock back, and so "tomorrow's people" then become "yesterday's people". As they get older they sigh for the good old days of their youth, and repeat the fallacy which they once rejected that the "best days are the school days". Their butterfly minds and hearts cannot rest long enough in the present to enjoy life, and so they are perpetually restless. The past eventually is so idealized that it becomes the source of discontent with the present. "It never happened in my days" and "the world is going to the dogs" is their constant complaint because they fail to realize that "my day" is today, and that when we change the world changes with us.

"Tomorrow's people" when they are young accelerate too fast for their age, and so miss out on their youth, until eventually they live their older years in reverse gear as "yesterday's people". They often try to recapture their lost youth, and so never know the real thrill of living each day to the full, with the quality of peace that it brings. Their past and their future destroy their present. We have to be of our age and our time every moment of our lives if we want true peace.

Many church-goers are among "yesterday's" and "tomorrow's" people because they never allow themselves or their churches the luxury of taking the risks of living to the full in the present. They decide that it is better to "hasten slowly" in order to make the minimum of mistakes, and so deprive their young followers of the joy of the Christian challenge of today. There is little joy in the Christian churches which do not live in the present, and so their young are lost because their "time has not yet come". Who has the right to say so, and why do we still wonder why our congregations are middle-aged? Jesus would have a field day among church leaders asking the questions: "Why are you afraid?" "Why is it that you have no faith?" The churches and world need the leadership of "today's people" to take their followers each day like pilgrims into uncharted territory. Christian leadership requires a boldness which makes us live out the present moment to the full, since the present moment alone will always remain our only hope for the future, our gratitude for the past and our peace for the present.

True Christians are "today's people" who can face up to every problem because they believe that God is with them in all their difficulties. He has not promised to solve their problems but to be with them through every situation in which they find themselves. They have sufferings in the past and aspirations for the future, but they commit them all into the hands of a loving God who is their Father and who knows what is best for them. They are a joy to live with, and every moment throbs with life and vitality because they have discovered the secret of living in the reality of the present. They are for ever young in their spirit of joy and wonder at life.

They truly follow Jesus, to whose life they will constantly return for inspiration. He was a man for all seasons and of their time, because he was fully of his own. He was so taken up with every "now" that he never made elaborate plans for even the most dramatic moments of his life. He left the "choreography" and "stage management" to his Father, and so a borrowed upper room and a borrowed cross provided the perfect setting for the Last Supper and his death, which no amount of human planning could dare to emulate. The *only* way to find true peace of soul, says Jesus, is to live in the present. In this way, even though their life style may be disturbed, Christians will always be at peace. They develop a philosophy of life which blesses them with a wisdom and peace which the world cannot give and will never fully understand.

As Christians they are at peace because they have in Jesus surrendered their lives to God, and always know (believe) that they are where they should be. Because they are "poor in spirit" they have not planned their lives, or schemed for their own benefit, so that whatever happens to them in the world is God's will. They use suffering creatively so that when sorrows come their way they will remember Jesus' words: "I tell you most solemnly, you will be weeping and wailing while the world will rejoice, you will be sorrowful but your sorrow will be turned into joy" (John 16:20). "Today's people" know that sorrow will pass and joy will come in the Lord's good time. Even in the midst of apparent disaster, they still go forward living out the "now". This is their secret weapon which destroys worry and brings them peace. Each day has enough troubles of its own, but also its peace for the Christian. My constant prayer for years has been, "One day at a time, Lord Jesus; one day at a time."

6

Growing Through Friendship

Love

"What I command you," said Jesus, "is to love one another" (John 15:17). This looks easy at first glance, but is it? To love as a Christian should be one of the most disturbing and fulfilling things in my life. Without it peace is impossible. The poorest person in the world is the one who has no friends. My life has been blessed with true, deep, lasting friendships. At each critical stage in my life, my friends have shared deeply with me, and helped me to grow as a person. I am today what they have offered me of themselves, so that I was able along the way to face life with the renewed strength and vision they gave me. Such deep friendships are rare, because it is the quality of friendship which counts rather than the number of friends with which I surround myself. Yet there have been times when some of my friendships have gone wrong, and I have retired bruised from the encounter. Like everyone else, I am more vulnerable to my friends than to anyone else. So as a Christian I have to ask myself the questions: What do I mean by "Christian friendship"? Why do some of my friendships, so rich in promise, sometimes fail? Why do they disturb me and so often threaten my peace? How can I develop gospel peace in my life through deep Christian friendship?

The reason why some of my friendships fail is because basically I am selfish in my dealings with others. Because I am still growing in my understanding of what "Christian love" (friendship) involves, I am bound even now to fail in some of my attempts at friendship. Nevertheless I must be honest enough to ask myself the question "Why?" My failed friendships were born out of my own selfish need to be loved, rather than out of a desire to give something of myself to my friend. I suppose the giving at the time filled a need within myself to feel wanted. True love is simple and straightforward, but because of the effects of sin I am a very strange, complicated person of mixed emotions and motivations. The "Christian self" and the "selfish self" are in conflict, especially in friendship. It takes a lifetime to unravel the mystery of self and to distinguish between what is real or false love, between love which is God-centred and that which is self-centred. It is said that the only passport to heaven is love. I believe it is also the only valid one on the earth. The knowledge that only God can love in me and that he needs me to love in, is a truth which is basic to my life as a Christian. It dominates my attitude to life and to people. If I love as a Christian should, then those who know me well should be drawn to the Christian faith because love has an irresistible attraction of its own. "Try then," says St Paul, "to imitate God, as children of his that he loves, and follow Christ by loving as he loved you" (Ephesians 5:1).

People have their surfeit of systems and ideologies which speak of "peace" and "love", when all they want is to see love in action in you and me and those who call themselves Christians. When I look on love as a gift from God which is to be passed on as part of my Christian vocation, then I must use it as an indispensable force in Christian mission for the peace and unity of the world in which I live. I look on people as a gift and not a threat, "for God's Holy Spirit, God's gift, does not want you to be afraid of people, but to be wise and strong, and to love them and to enjoy being with them" (2 Timothy 1:7). I love being with people, and see it as one of the greatest joys of my Christian life. In recent years the Maranatha Community, of which I am a co-founder, has brought me great Christian love and helped me to love others. It is a source of great strength and healing because it is a sharing in Christian love.

People, in their turn, are attracted by Christian love as by a magnet, not because of what we consciously do or say but because of something indefinable within us which makes us different. This mysterious force within us is a love which excludes no one from its warmth. When I live a full Christian life of love then I am helping others to lead their lives as fully as possible. "You must all think of what is best for each other and for the community. Be happy at all times . . . because this is what God expects you to do in Christ Jesus" (1 Thessalonians 5:15–18).

I am not pretending it is easy to live up to the demands of Jesus' gospel of friendship, and so I turn to his life style to understand what true Christian friendship really means. He knew the pain of loving with little return, yet he was always perfectly at peace in the depth of his soul, because he was at peace with God his Father. This was the foundation on which he built all his friendships. When friendships went wrong it was never his fault. He loved his own people even when they turned against him and wanted him crucified. Among his closest followers there was scant return in loving friendship because of their shallow understanding of what true friendship really means. Judas, reprimanded by Jesus over a simple matter of a box of ointment, sold him cheaply to his enemies. Even at the moment of betrayal Jesus still called Judas "friend" (Matthew 26:50), because as a true friend he had already forgiven Judas for what he had done. Jesus had few friends who proved themselves when it really mattered. His closest friends fell asleep when he was undergoing his severest test of faith and courage in

Gethsemane. His chosen leader, Peter, denied him three times. What is more depressing than to be let down in a moment of crisis by your friends whom you rely on? You expect rejection from your enemies but not from your friends, and this is the real test of love when you carry on calling them friends because this is what they will always remain to you. It is in the rejection of my offer of friendship that the quality of my Christian love is being tested. It is easy to be a fair-weather friend, but the crunch comes when there is nothing to be gained from the friendship, when my friend gets everything from the relationship leaving me apparently with nothing.

Jesus was a friend to everyone, even his enemies, and as the example of *the perfect friend* he shows us through his life style that all Christian friendship is rooted in God, the Father. The moment I exclude God from my friendship then things will start to go wrong. Ernesto Cardenal says that "Love is someone else dwelling within our person. Love is a presence. It is feeling we belong to someone else and that someone else belongs to us." We belong to God in a way in which we cannot belong to anyone else. This is the simple yet demanding criterion of Christian love (friendship).

No human being can ever be my *total* happiness in this life, because, as St Augustine says, "You have made us for yourself, O Lord; restless are our hearts until they rest in Thee." If I want full peace then I must give my total love to God alone. Once I surrender this total love to others then I make a "god" of them, and they disturb my inner peace because they usurp God's rightful place in my mind, heart and soul. "You must love the Lord your God," said Jesus, "with all your heart, with all your soul, and with all your mind" (Matthew 22:37). It is round this *total* loving of God that the whole difficulty of Christian loving revolves.

A young couple who were very happy in their marriage

gave me an insight into this kind of Christian love. They were exceptionally dedicated Christians and obviously deeply in love with each other. I came to know them very well, and one day asked them the secret of their happiness. They told me that the depth of their love came from their mutual love of God and that it was this love which drew them so close to each other in marriage. I found this quite an extraordinary way of looking at love. Tragically the husband died at an early age from a rare disease, and his young widow cried in sorrow at her loss. I was among her many close friends who tried to console her, but it was obvious that there was a hidden force greater than us all supporting and strengthening her. She told us in her own quiet way that she wanted to be alone with God so that he could explain why things had happened the way they had. After a period of grief it was obvious to us all that she understood quite wonderfully what God's will was for her at that particular period in her life. I have never seen anyone grow out of such a situation in such a beautiful way. She was a good woman before the tragedy: she was a better Christian after it because she used her sorrow to grow in peace. Christian love, when it is expressed like this, gives me a glimpse of what God's love is really like.

The love of God and the love of my neighbour (friend) are for me as a Christian inextricably intertwined. The one involves the other: "A man who does not love the brother that he can see cannot love God whom he has never seen" (John 4:20). It is tragic that there are so few who understand what Christian love means. Our world has trivialized it and taught people to live by its counterfeit. From my own experience as a priest I know that there are many people in our love-starved world who smile on the outside and pretend they are happy, but feel the gnawing emptiness within. They have an inner loveless emptiness and are not at inner peace because merely human love can never reach the inner recesses of their soul: they need something more. It is this special deep inner love which made the young wife proclaim that she loved her husband so beautifully because she saw that love set into her love of God, who could alone claim her total love. Idealistic though it may seem, true Christian friendship always points beyond itself. When it ends with us then it is already doomed. It slips back into the mortal, merely human, and loses the eternal because the divine spark is not in it.

The "other" for us as Christians in total love, is God the Father. Even in marriage, it is wrong to say to the other person "You are my *total* happiness" since no human being can stand in that exclusive relationship to another. When the marriage fails, because of the selfish element in our imperfect love, we may blame the other for not being what we expected them to be, whereas the fault lies deep within ourselves because of our false idea of love. We had no right to make the demand for total happiness from others in the first place, since there is no possibility of its being fulfilled in such a total way.

The reason why friendships fail is basically because, without realizing it, we have through selfishness tended to manipulate and possess our friends for our own selfish ends. The selfish part of ourselves has dominated the relationship, and the selfish love, which has not centred itself on "the other" but on "self", instead of being a gift becomes a threat. We all have met selfish people. What a tragic figure such a person is. He lives his life surrounded by people who are mere acquaintances, but will remain bereft of friends. His path takes him across a desert which he himself has made. He will at times see mirages of friendship which will disappear as soon as reality reasserts itself. He has refused to be himself, and to offer the most precious commodity of self to another. Many successful people, by the world's standards, are lonely deep inside themselves because love for them has a low priority in their scheme of things. Power and true friendship rarely coexist, because power people are not sufficiently poor in spirit to acknowledge their need of friendship or give sufficient time to allow friendship to grow and develop. Power is their substitute for true friends, and makes for loneliness.

A truly deep friendship can only exist by letting the other person be "other", just as God allows us to be "other" to him. It takes a lifetime for a friend to grow side by side to ourselves, so that the closer two friends become, the more the mystery of "the other" grows. To know a person well in true friendship is to acknowledge that there is always more to be known about them. From experience I know that it is through my very closest friends that I am beginning to understand what the love of God must be. It is through them that I grow as a Christian. The Maranatha Community has shown me what the big institutional churches should be, and what a force they could be for the spread of the Gospel once love is to the forefront of our attitude to one another.

I have been blessed with a truly happy childhood in a loving home. The natural place for our spiritual and emotional growth in friendship is in the setting of the family where we learn to relate to our parents, brothers and sisters so that through them we are equipped to deal with people in a wider context. Unfortunately the experience of many people who are damaged in their emotional lives is of unhappiness, selfishness and insecurity in their home background. Typical of many such cases of this destructive love is that of a selfish mother I knew who believed that her whole family revolved round her. It was her husband, who stayed quietly in the background, who was the real heart and centre of the family. When he died her whole selfish world collapsed like a pack of cards. Her possessive love was such that she considered the love given to her by her husband and children was hers by right. Even the sympathy in her family's bereavement was wholly directed towards herself.

She lived in an illusion of how wonderful she was as a mother, whereas her children regarded her as a selfish tyrant who dominated their lives. When they were old enough they went their own ways without any regrets, leaving her to walk alone in her empty house which she never allowed to become a home. She became a pathetic figure with whom it was extremely difficult to communicate, as she grumbled incessantly about how unfair life had been to her and refused to accept that there was any fault on her part. Friends, who used to call in the past to see the family (in reality to meet the husband), avoided her like the plague, and so became an addition to her litany of complaints. She had failed to realize how selfish she had been as a mother and, now widowed without her family round her, she could not bear to face up to herself. She is one of the loneliest people I know and however much I try, I have never been able to make real deep contact with her. Today some of her children are still bitter about their young days and are complete misfits in society.

In so-called Christian homes I have met many psychologically mutilated people who have turned their backs on God and every form of human friendship, and all because they were the victims of a completely possessive, selfish relationship within the family circle. Because there is no love in their homes they are unable to look on God as a Father. There are unmarried daughters, for example, who have sacrificed themselves for their families out of an exaggerated sense of Christian duty and loyalty, while knowing in their hearts that they were being manipulated by a selfish parent. It is all very well to comfort them with the thought that they will get their reward in the next life, but what about this one? Unable psychologically to break the fetters which bound them to the demanding personality of a widowed or emotionally deprived parent, they became the one who stayed at home whether they liked it or not. They missed out on inner peace and personal fulfilment, and ultimately grew to hate the person who kept them a prisoner of the home. "Parents," warns St Paul, "never drive your children to resentment" (Ephesians 6:4).

If a happy family background is necessary for an early training in Christian friendship, then what is one to say of divorce? My first experience of a divorce case was shattering. I heard the husband and wife in court blame each other bitterly for the breakdown of the marriage, and quarrel selfishly about the custody of the children. The children were in fact the victims of this unfortunate couple, who had repudiated their marriage vows and had left each other with the sour taste of a shared life which ended in hatred. As she left the courtroom the wife spat the words at her husband: "If I never see you again it will be too soon," while he, completely ignoring her, departed on the arm of his new "love". It was hurtful to realize that only five years previously I had celebrated the Mass in which they promised before God to love "until death", and everyone present on that occasion said that their marriage "was made in heaven" because they were such a loving couple! Many good Christians, too, are driven to seek separation from their spouses because of their selfishness and false chauvinistic attitude which never allowed the other person space to breathe or to become themselves.

These are but a few of the instances of the wrong kinds of human relationships which destroy our inner peace because they hold us back from loving God and our neighbour which is our duty and privilege. If friendship is a "reaching out" to the other, and this is denied us by those closest to us, then we are condemned to a closed-in, loveless life. There are many tragic figures in the world who limp through their existence, and sometimes take refuge in religion. They will never allow God to touch the depths of their soul because they are incapable of any form of relationship. They blame everyone else but themselves for their failure in human relationships. The wine of human love has gone sour for them and its vinegary taste distorts every other form of love. Peace has not rested in their souls for many years, and they "hassle" others because of their own restless selfishness.

I mention these forms of disastrous friendships because they help to make me realize how blessed I have been in my life with family and friends. Even still, making deep Christian friendships, which lead me to God because he is in them already, is a very demanding experience. I suppose, mindful of the mistakes and hurts of the past, I shall always remain to some extent basically afraid to make friends I am afraid to love and let go of myself in "the other" because I shall of necessity be changed by "the other" in the relationship. Despite my Christian belief and experience, my "selfish self" tells my "Christian self" that when I love then I am no longer in sole control of my time and interests. I am afraid that I may lose something of my "selfish self", to which in some weird way I shall always instinctively and possessively cling. Peace through friendship is a risk which I have to take if I want to know true, inner, gospel peace.

Being a Christian does not minimize my human feelings and attitudes, and so I know that in every true friendship I risk being hurt because through it I offer myself as I am to others, and this makes me vulnerable to them. This means that through the change in myself involved in friendship, I am as liable to be subject to pain and loss as to joy and discovery. Who willingly wants to suffer pain unless he understands it as creative and necessary for his growth in inner peace? And yet this is what true friendship always entails. Fear of the unknown factors in friendship involving a real change in myself often destroys my growth in friendship with God and my neighbour because it holds me back through selfishness from going out to "the other" in selflessness. This fear has to be healed and I have witnessed many instances of it in the Maranatha Community. Jesus submitted himself to change through his friends, yet I am even now afraid of being changed because it is a form of dying to what I am. Instinctively I am tempted to put limits on my "friendship offer". My motto is "thus far and no further" because I am afraid to take the risk of being hurt. My peace is an uneasy truce when I am not sure of what is involved.

Yet as a Christian I know that no one, not even my enemies, is to be excluded from my "friendship". This is the disturbing element in Jesus' command "to love one another". However, I shall go on trying to be at peace and friendship with everyone because this is what Jesus demands of me. I can no longer pick and choose my friends, once I choose to follow the life style of Jesus and desire to experience his peace. It will always be through people that I shall come to know and serve God. I bless all those friends in my life who have given me the inspiration and courage to look out on my world, and see in it the warm glow of a redeemed friendship. The one friend who made it possible for us all to be friends is God's Son, who took human flesh so that our human love would be touched with the divine. He no longer calls us "servants but friends" (John 15:15). No matter how disturbing a friendship may seem to be, I shall always continue to seek in it his presence and his peace.

7

Being Prepared To Love Your Enemies

Forgiveness

Most people find it hard to forgive those who have injured them. Yet until we do we will never be true Christians or experience gospel peace. Jesus is uncompromising about friendship: "If you love those who love you," he said, "what right have you to claim any credit? Even the tax collectors do as much, do they not? And if you save your greetings for your brothers, are you doing anything exceptional? Even the pagans do as much, do they not?" (Matthew 5:47). To whom then does my Christian friendship extend? Has it any limits? To everyone, said Jesus, even your enemies, because God is the Father of us all. "You have learnt how it was said: You must love your neighbour and hate your enemy. But I say this to you: Love your enemies. In this way you will be sons of your Father in heaven for he causes his sun to rise on bad men as well as good" (Matthew 5:43–45). This "loving your enemies" and being prepared to love everyone seems disruptive of my peace. In practice I find it extremely difficult, if not impossible, to follow this philosophy of open-ended friendship in my daily life. As a rule I tend to love only those who love me. I like the "goodies" of this world, and am tempted to turn my back on the "baddies", leaving them to their own devices. I find it hard enough to be friendly to my friends without having to cope with my enemies as well. "I love you" is a return I give to the person who loves me, a quid pro quo in the weighing scales of friendship, so that in merely human terms I am prepared to give only in so far as I receive.

If I were not a Christian I would be exclusive and limiting in my love, and just about back "even money" on the roulette table of human relationships. I would not take too big a chance because I am afraid to take a risky gamble on such a precious thing as love, with its terrible consequences if I lose. Yet every friendship is a gamble and adventure, as in my life I watch the gaming wheel turn through people and situations in which I find myself. Once I dare to love I shall no longer have sole control over the result; it is too late for me to withdraw my bet. In human love there is gain only where there is the risk of loss. If this is true of my friends, then what of my enemies? Surely the risk is too great with only an outside chance of winning. Does Jesus really want me to love my enemies or is it an exaggeration on his part in order to show me how perfect God's love is? I could not even attempt to love like that; or must I, if I want to be a Christian and experience his gospel peace? Jesus thought so because he said: "You must therefore be perfect just as your heavenly Father is perfect" (Matthew 5:48).

As a damaged person I am basically selfish and if left to myself and my own feelings, despite my highest Christian ideals, the first type of love which invariably dominates my emotions is "selfish love". I want to love people who love me, rather than to love them with nothing in return. That is why, when I am presented with the ideal of Christian friendship for my enemies, I invariably shortcircuit such unselfish love with the question, "What is in it for me?" Whether I am a Christian or not, my damaged nature remains the same, and I am still afraid to be unselfish. Selfish love is part and parcel of who I am in the "here and now", and it is very damaging and unrealistic to pretend otherwise. In common parlance, loving your enemies is "not on" if such a friendship is to be weighed in purely human emotional terms. Enemies by definition seek our destruction and are not for our peace.

Yet selfish love is of its nature self-destructive in the final analysis because it turns me in on myself instead of outwards to other people. Just as there is no painless way of truly loving my friends, and no other way of growing as a person, then how much more spiritually fruitful it is if no one, even my enemy, is excluded from my friendship. If I want to live the Christian life according to its full gospel message then I shall soon discover that loving my enemies is a command of Jesus which I must take seriously and literally.

"We never really love," says Jesus, "if we do so only in the hope of return", and yet love of our enemies does not seem at first sight to be very practical advice. Loving our enemies is in fact the only way to true fulfilling peace, because then no one is able to disturb our deep peace of soul. To the extent that anyone is excluded from our love then our inner peace is correspondingly diminished because such a person makes us unpeaceful. It is my enemies who exclude me from their friendship. I am their enemy; they are not mine. When I truly love others for themselves and they do not return my love, then it is they who are the losers, whereas I know that through the unreturned friendship my capacity to love is increased. My "friends" may never know that through them I experienced a dying, and a growth in loving, because they did not appreciate that it was friendship which was being offered. They did not understand my Christian love because they had never experienced it in their own lives. Like Jesus the only thing left for me is to commend my love of them to God my Father, which is the greatest thing I can do with any friendship. Through this Christian approach to love and friendship, especially of my enemies, there have been times when I have discovered an inner peace in my own life which people saturated with the narrowness of the materialistic world's vision of love do not think possible. Once we truly forgive someone who has hurt us however grievously then they can never hurt us again. Much of the healing in our Maranatha Community has been directed to helping people forgive those nearest and dearest to them who have hurt them.

But how does this rejection of my offer of friendship help me to grow in Christian peace and commitment? Surely it will only make me bitter or look a fool if I go on loving like this? True Christian love, like all love, cannot stand still, and each encounter in selfless love with another is a step forward in my growth towards becoming an integrated person. If I suffer rejection by someone and my hurt feelings predominate, then of course I am tempted to retire behind my wounds resolved never to love again. After all, why should I forgive a hurt for which there seemed no reason? If, however, I have indeed truly loved as a Christian, the test of my friendship will be whether or not I shall go forward on the road to even deeper Christian love in the future. If I do then I shall know that I have offered friendship for its own sake and not in the hope of return.

It is once again the paradox of dying to my "selfish self" in order to live the true life of my "Christian self". No one can stop us from loving like this if we too have the mind of Jesus and ask for his inspiration and help. The rejection of Jesus by his own people will always remain the perfect example for me of what true, unselfish love really means. He never stopped loving his enemies right to the end, and his last words on the Cross were a plea to his Father to *forgive* them. Their rejection of him merely highlights his total love. He gives me his peace when I too give others my love as he gave his. I know from bitter experience how often I fall short of this ideal in practice. There are some people who are so hostile to me and my beliefs – they do not consider me a Christian – that for sanity's sake, if for no other reason, I am forced to withdraw from them the "privilege of contact" while still commending them in all sincerity to the Lord.

Failure truly to love others because of my fear of being rejected makes me realize that my love is still very selfish. Just as a rose bush constantly needs pruning of its suckers, so love of "selfish self" must be cut out of our lives because it saps our capacity for deep and unselfish sharing of ourselves with others. At each encounter, whether of acceptance or rejection of the friendship I offer to another, I have to come to terms with myself in the depths of my personality and question the motivation of my love. Perhaps for the first time in my life, when I experienced rejection, I was able to see myself as I really was, not only in relation to my enemies but to those whom I considered to be my friends. I realized how much support I expected from them and how dependent on them I had become over the years, to the point of taking them for granted. Friendship that is not renewed frequently soon dies.

I have to ask myself the following questions in every friendship. "Is my offer genuine and sincere? Am I for the other's peace and growth as a person? Do I really love the other for his sake alone, or how much selfishness is involved in my loving? How much would I be hurt if the friendship came apart at the seams, and how much therefore am I prepared to risk of myself and of my inner peace in the gamble of love? Would I continue to love him if he rejected my friendship?" Only time will provide the answer to these questions, but the saying is still true, especially for the Christian, that "it is better to have loved and lost than never to have loved at all".

Because there have been times when I have been hurt in a

friendship which I valued greatly, the temptation will always remain that I shall cut my losses short and so be afraid to trust myself again with the same openness and confidence to other people. I shall be tempted to put up barriers and retire behind my "protectively padded self". Yet it is through the creative use of every relationship, however hurtful it may be to my feelings and disturbing to my peace, that I learn to grow as a full person. Christian love at its purest will always turn a situation which fosters hatred and bitterness into a motive for loving even more, even finding excuses for those who reject us. I have seen people time and again forgive those who hurt them, only to see their friendship spurned. I remember a mother in my first parish who was consistently beaten by her drunken son and yet every time she forgave him. "He may not be a good son," she said, "but that does not excuse me from not trying to be a good mother." She was one of the saints in my life who has long since gone to her reward.

The strange paradox is that we grow spiritually through painful relationships just as much, if not more, than through joyful ones. Dryden reminds us in Eleonora: "For friendship, of itself a holy tie, is made more sacred by adversity." Jesus, abandoned by his Apostles during his Passion, was at that very time closest to his Father. It often takes the pain of indifference, betrayal or denial by friends to make us turn completely to God alone who is our true friend, and friendships deepest meaning. He is our Father who will never desert us in our times of trial. If I learn to surrender all my friendships to him then nothing in my human relationships can ever destroy me.

When I look back over my life I find, however, that I have not been very successful in loving my enemies. In fact, my training for the priesthood was not very helpful in this respect. In my seminary days I was instructed in a weird philosophy concerning those students with whom I failed to establish any meaningful form of deep comradeship. My spiritual directors at college consoled me with a facile distinction that while Jesus told us to "love" everyone he did not mention any obligation to "like" them. So I went on my way blissfully liking those who liked me, and relegating those whom I disliked to the periphery of my life. I was content to "love" them in a vague way which cost me nothing. There were some students with whom I shared the same roof for many years but with whom I never had any deep conversation, and I am sure the fault was at least partly mine. This was not done so much deliberately, except in so far as I opted to belong to a group of friends who had similar interests to mine. It never even occurred to me that I had any obligation even to attempt to like everyone, and what I was not obliged to do just did not get done. Even though my seminary gave me so much, and I love it as very much part of me, nevertheless in the late forties there were more important rules to be observed in a seminary for training priests than friendliness and sharing, and yet we were to be the future Christian leaders of our people! In those far-off unecumenical days we had it instilled into us that as Roman Catholics we were right and other Christian Churches wrong, and we were taught, of course, that "error has no rights". How unChristian this attitude is, and yet how doggedly it persists in the lives of so many clergy until it ultimately destroys their inner peace as individual Christians and Churches and holds them back from growth as full persons, and full communities united in love and peace.

In my search for gospel peace I have no option as a Christian but to love and to strive hard to like everyone, irrespective of class, colour or creed. If in return they do not reciprocate my Christian love I cannot excuse myself from living out my friendship to everyone. The main point for me is that I continue to treat them as my brothers and sisters, and this will remain my duty and calling even though it is made more difficult, especially when Christians of different Churches do not even begin to love one another. Some Protestants in Northern Ireland, for example, may reject me out of hand because I am a Catholic priest, but my response is to show them that I am a Christian, and not just a Catholic, by my love for them, and that they have nothing to fear from me. Catholics, on the other hand, may feel that my criticism of my Church is a personal attack on their established way of thinking and see me as a threat. Even though I try to love them as a Christian should I am *saddened* that they will not give me the opportunity to come closer to their lives so that we can get to know and understand each other better. If we cannot disagree and remain true brothers and sisters in the love of Jesus then what is the point of belonging to a Church which is divisive and sectarian?

What is true of individuals in their Churches is also true on the wider scale of Christian communities. When both groups, Catholic and Protestant, reject each other without true dialogue, which leaves both parties open to change and growth, then confrontation is imminent. This is the sadness in Northern Ireland of such otherwise wonderfully caring people and Church leaders. They become "enemies" not because of their own personal choosing, but because their background has deprived them of looking at each other in complete, honest, Christian love. The dice are loaded against them from the outset, and the seeds of peace lie fallow in the desert of distrust.

Sadness at human divisions between individuals and communities is, I think, a sign from God our Father that we want in our hearts to draw closer to people and to have them as friends, even though they may still regard us as their enemies. We may never say like the Pharisee, "Thank God I am not one of them." Jesus wept over the people of

Jerusalem, and for me the lack of genuine love in and between the Churches is a deep sadness which I and many ecumenically orientated people have to bear. Yet the sufferings I and others endure is for the sake of future peace and unity. There are cynics who claim that love went out of the ecclesiastical window at the Reformation and who dares to say that there is no truth in it? When as Christians we look on each other in love which accepts our differences, then God's love will again take flesh and live among us and the Gospel of unity will be more effectively preached. The Spirit of love will also heal the wounds of division between the Churches and bring them the healing peace of unity in love. We cannot do it if we are left to our own resources. If we ignore the command of Christ, "This is my commandment: *love one another as I have loved you*" (John 15:12), then Catholics and Protestants will go their own separate ways with increasing barriers of distrust between them. They will certainly not be Christian in the gospel sense of the word, and their peace, like their love, will be limited and limiting.

If we genuinely believe that through the gift of the Holy Spirit at baptism Christians become one with the risen Jesus, surely we will not only overcome our human distrust of each other but we will love each other in the way he did. He will be once again the unifying force in our lives and our Churches, the sign of peace and unity by which everyone will know we are his disciples. "May they all be one. *Father, may they be one in us*, as you are in me and I am in you, *so that the world may believe it was you who sent me*" (John 17:21). Christian love, like prayer, can only be learned by practice, and I find it hard to practise this form of selfless love, especially when I cannot see any immediate visible progress. Yet it will always remain for me the only form of living a meaningful Christian life in a frighteningly loveless and divided world and Church. If I trust God as a

Father and commit my life and Church to him, he will reward my efforts in a way he knows best. His gift to me even now is the first Christmas message of "peace to all", whether they are of good will or not, because in my heart no one is my enemy.

Because the barriers of distrust have to be loved away rather than broken down we must be prepared to be misunderstood. It is only when we see the other person's point of view *from* his point of view that gradually our Christian love will foster mutual trust and forgiveness. Christian love makes no distinction between loving friends and enemies. It is all part of my Christian love of myself in the best possible way. Meister Eckhart writes: "If you love yourself, you love everybody else as you do yourself. As long as you love another person more than you love yourself, you will not really succeed in loving yourself, but if you love all alike, including yourself, you will love them as one person and that one person is both God and man." If I love anyone less than myself or more than myself, then I shall not be able to love them or myself as Jesus wants. My love of God is reflected in the light of his love which shines on everyone with equal brightness.

In the final analysis it is Christ's love and life in me which casts out all my fear and distrust and brings me peace. I have always felt that the words of Desiderata have special significance for the Christian: "Be at peace with God whatever you conceive him to be, and whatever your labours and aspirations in the noisy confusion of life, keep peace with your soul. With all its sham and drudgery and broken dreams, it is still a beautiful world." I become a real peacemaker for the world when I make peace with everyone in my world through Christian love, the world I know, and with which I come in daily contact. This is my mission and challenge today and every day, but I must "First make peace with myself," says St Ambrose, "so that when I have become peaceful I may bring peace to others." *The peace inside me when I really love my enemies helps to bring peace to everyone around me*. When the risen Christ said "peace be with you" to his Apostles, he called them and all his followers not only to be at peace but also to *make peace*.

I bring Christ's peace to a world in conflict, and a Church divided, when I live my life in union with the reconciling death and resurrection of God's Son. No one is to be my enemy and I am not afraid to make friends with peoples of all faiths and none because the love of Christ's spirit lives in me. "For he [Christ] is the peace between us and has made the two into one, and broken down the barrier which used to keep them (us) apart" (Ephesians 2:14). I will only become the instrument of my neighbour's peace when, even though I am his enemy, I am still prepared to be his friend and pay the price for it.

8

Growing Through Creative Silence

Prayer

The wish is father to the thought. This is often the case with me. Take silence for example. How many times have I said in the middle of a busy day, "Oh, if only I had some time to myself for peace and quiet!" Yet in my younger days when I had the opportunity to be silent I did not know how to use it. While desiring to be alone I was afraid of it. Today I have become much wiser, and deeply value the moments of creative silence which take me into a deeper awareness of the presence of God and his peace.

What is true of me is also true of modern society. If I want to find true Christian peace then I must develop this contemplative side of my life, because what God says to me is much more important than anything I could say to him. Yet I am a product of the frenetically noisy society in which I live, and this is why I have had to cultivate the art of creative silence. And what a crazy society it is! Our youth go to discotheques where the music is turned up so loudly that they cannot hear each other talk, and the lights are dimmed so that they cannot see each other, and they call it "entertainment"! In many homes the television set is perpetually turned on – in some homes I have seen it used as light for a darkened room – and the record player is blaring out its strident "top pop twenty" to which no one listens. Everything is done to the sound of music at our places of work, with the emphasis on sound rather than music, thus making our age, with all its modern gadgets of instant communication, an age where dialogue is practically physically impossible. Is it any wonder that so many people talk for the sake of sound, but true conversation is non-existent? I am constantly in danger of becoming drugged by noise which prevents me from really thinking about life and its meaning. Modern society does not seem to know what inner peace means, and so it careers inevitably on its way to disintegration of individuals and families, dragging me along with it.

It is difficult to be a Christian amid all this noise and emptiness unless I fill myself with God's presence. It is through the life style of Jesus that I begin to understand what prayer is, and how necessary it is for me to learn the value of silence. The more I read the Gospel the more I am convinced of the need for a hidden life with God because through this I become more attuned to the life style of Jesus. Luke describes how, when he left the temple at the age of twelve, he went down to Nazareth where for the next eighteen years he "grew in age and wisdom before men and God" (Luke 2:40). This means that Jesus grew within himself spiritually during that hidden time as he was being prepared and was preparing himself for his public ministry. When I say that Jesus grew in his inner life I am merely stating that while he always prayed perfectly according to the circumstances in which he was placed, nevertheless when he was a child he prayed as a child and there was room for his prayer life to grow and develop. He needed the eighteen years away from the world's gaze so that in his periods of silence he could grow into the kind of man who could endure so lovingly the terrible agony of his crucifixion. After all it was a man and not a boy who died on a cross. Would a boy have understood the enormity of the sufferings or, more important, would we? The night before his crucifixion he experienced all the adult fears of dying which only a fully grown, sensitive person could appreciate in the precise way he did. The man Jesus knew what it was all about and the price in suffering he would have to pay for loving his Father. If Jesus needed the seclusion of Nazareth for so many years, then so do I if I am to live as a Christian in my world. I, like Jesus, will grow to love God through silence and a hidden life with him. It is the best preparation I can have for living as an evangelist intent on proclaiming Christ's Gospel.

But what is the value of the hidden life with God and silence? Surely I must go out into the world and use words if I want to communicate, or else remain isolated from the world? What about witnessing to Christ in the world? Only those who know the value of silence, and the need at times to be alone, have a true reverence for words. They alone are equipped for meaningful conversation and Christian witness which flow from reflective conviction, so that what they say has the ring of authority about it. I would rather listen to one sentence from a holy monk than hear a lecture from an intelligent, over-active professor. As Jesus moved towards the end of his life he used words less and less. He was silent before his accusers at his trial, and his few sentences from the Cross are among the most treasured in the Bible. I wonder what would happen if he walked into one of our noisy cocktail parties today, with their meaningless shallow chatter. He would probably reduce everyone to silence, and when he left the noise of "conversation" would erupt again like a jumbo jet setting off at dawn over a sleeping city.

The Christian churches have suffered in the West because they too seem to have forgotten the value of silence for those who seek inner Christian peace. In their emphasis on action they have underestimated the value of the "hidden self" in which we appreciate people for what they are rather than what they say. In the Maranatha Community all our meetings include a period of deep silence. The Eastern churches and mystics have a lot to offer us on the value of meditation, and the Jesus Prayer is a typical example of the power of reflective prayer. The closer I come to understanding my real "inner self" in prayer, the more I am able to enter into the mood of creative silence which takes me into the pain and turmoil of the world around me, and ultimately into its peace. It is here that, paradoxically, silence disturbs me and brings me peace.

But how can I learn to be silent in a world suffocated by noise? Just as conversation, to be meaningful, must flow from deep within us, so also we have to prepare ourselves for what we do with silence when we encounter it. The first thing to remember is that the *place* for silence is important. It sets the mood for contemplation. For example, when I sit watching a river flow by I am opening myself to nature and its beauty. I see myself more and more then as part of God's wonderful creation and in the process find it easier to pray and think. The same trend of going apart to pray runs all through Jesus' life, and he tells me time and again in his preaching that a silent place in which to pray is the perfect setting for the music and language of my peace of soul.

Whenever he was faced with a difficult decision to make, or needed some time by himself to recharge his spiritual batteries, he sought a quiet place where he could be alone without any physical distractions. The night before he was crucified he withdrew to the garden of Gethsemane so that he could see the issues at stake more clearly, and come to a resolute decision. When he had spent a whole day healing the sick in Capernaum, and needed a rest, we read that, "In the morning, long before dawn, he got up and left the house, and went off to a lonely place and prayed there" (Mark 1:35). He tells us too, "When you pray, go to your private room and when you have shut your door, pray to your Father who is in that secret place" (Matthew 6:6).

Jesus knew only too well the value of creative silence, and as I grow in an awareness of God's presence I can shut out the noisy world no matter where I am. Mother Teresa's nuns in Calcutta can hardly hear the priest saying Mass because their convent is filled with the noise of passing trams. They have learned to love that noise so that it fits into their prayer life, but I am thinking in this book about lesser mortals, and how they can be silent in today's world.

The case of "Tom" is a typical example of the creative and restorative power of silence. When I first met him he was, in the eyes of the world, a "drop out", yet it was the restless and noisy society in which he lived which had destroyed him. He was only twenty-three but looked twice that age due to drugs, drink and a way of life which was aimless. He had been in and out of psychiatric hospitals, and it seemed that nothing could be done for him. I spent hours counselling him to no avail because he was unable to listen. Finally, almost in despair, I advised him to spend some time walking alone through the woods and sitting by the riverside at our pastoral centre. It worked wonders for him so that once again he found peace for his troubled spirit and a motive for real living. He was able to look at himself once he found the space within himself and his own spirit. He did not like what he saw but at least now he had a foundation for listening, and doing something positive about what he heard. Silence did much more for Tom than any words of advice which I gave him. He was just one of many helped by the peaceful surroundings of our centre set in one of Yorkshire's beautiful valleys. Nature was the peaceful setting on the outside which helped them to discover peace on the inside.

The life style of Jesus constantly reminds me that I must allow myself longer and deeper periods of silence if I am to become aware of the things in life that really matter. When I give myself space and time to think and pray in a relaxed setting, then I grow and mature as a Christian and, of course, as a person. People today are searching for the silence which brings peace of mind and soul, and so they flock in great numbers to monasteries and places where they know they will be given the facilities for reflection. What a marvellous opportunity for the churches to encourage contemplation. The more frenetic society becomes, the greater the need for me to find an island within myself where the noise is stilled and I can begin to experience the soothing balm of physical peace. We have so exaggerated John Donne's saying "no man is an island" that we forget that each of us has to find an island which belongs to ourselves alone where we can find time and space for reflection. The Jewish and Christian faiths, as well as many others, were born in the desert. From the beginning of time people have sought refuge in quiet places like deserts and mountains in order to discover deep within themselves the presence and the will of God, so that when they return to the world their lives and those whom they influence take on a new dimension. The best preparation for Christian witness to the world is to withdraw from it in order to seek the silence which speaks only of the presence of God and his will for the world.

Every Christian preaches himself and I am basically what I do with my silence. It is in silence, often in lonely places or situations, that God steals into my personality to talk to me in a way which is impossible even for my closest friends. They cannot help me to discover myself in the intimate way that God alone can. There have been times in my life when I have had to run away from people who, with all the good will in the world, wanted to help me yet the situation was beyond their scope. It was God alone who understood me and would help me to understand what the present situation meant, and what I must do about it. I have also had to allow God to take over in the lives and problems of those closest to me while I stood by and waited. He could do infinitely more for them than I could. Recently, I went to see a young mother who was very ill. She had very noisy visitors who kept up a pretence that all was well and the ward rang with their forced laughter. I could see that the patient laughed with her mouth but not with her eyes. When eventually they retired from her room, leaving her utterly exhausted, I sat and prayed with her, mostly in silence. She became totally relaxed and as I left the room I knew in some inexplicable way that she was experiencing the wonderful soothing peace of Christ. I had done my little part like an anaesthetist; the major spiritual surgery was best left in God's hands.

In over thirty years of priestly ministry I am more aware today than ever before that our noise-crazed world is crying out for meaningful silence which will help people to find an answer to the question about the meaning of life and inner peace. They want to hear about God because deep down in their souls they know they need him. As Christians we have in our time to learn again to speak to people quite simply about God and his love for them, but above all just *to be* to people and so make the reality of God come alive for them as well as for ourselves. When Jesus spoke to the Jews about his Father they listened as if they had heard it for the first time because everything he said had its authority flowing from his inner conviction. Holiness does not need words to proclaim its presence: it speaks for itself.

I have heard many eloquent sermons, but I always know the difference between the "professional" and the "preacher". With one the words come easily to the lips while the other finds his spirit is too full because the words he has are not enough. One of my parish priests was like that. He was not a very brilliant professional orator, but he was a very spiritual man. He had something indefinable about him which brought the presence of God wherever he went. He always sought places and times in the day when he could be alone with God to think and pray. When he died they mourned him deeply because he was a patently holy man and it was obvious that they loved him because, as they said, "his whole life was such a prayer that he didn't need to be or do anything else."

To seek silence in order to pray is necessary for me, because prayer, without words or at least not too many of them, far from being an escape from reality or the world, is in fact the special something which gives reality to my world. Jesus was anything but an escapist yet prayer in silent places was the number one priority in his life. I know from my own experience that when I try to go it alone without the prayer which is born out of silence, I soon become disturbed within myself and fall flat on my face. Left to my own human resources I am an easy prey for all sorts of irrational fears, but when I pray the prayer of listening to God I allow him to give something of his life and peace to me and my world.

And yet there are people in the Churches who are so obsessed with activities, and doing their "Martha role", that they are extremely critical of those who emphasize the need to be still and allow God to find us. The thousands of contemplative monks and nuns who devote their lives to prayer, and practically nothing else, are not above criticism from their fellow Christians. A very good Free Church woman came to Wood Hall Centre to visit the Carmelite Sisters, who spend most of their lives in prayer and silence. She expressed her dismay at seeing so many holy women wasting their lives locked up in a convent when they could be out in the world doing so much good. "You never *do* anything for anyone," she said, "all you do is pray and the world needs the witnesses of your good works as well." She had her priorities all wrong. Of course good works are necessary but she really believed that good works were more important than prayer, forgetting that no work is good unless it is the result of prayer. Surely the difference between a "do-gooder" and a Christian is the motivation for their work and the source of their activity.

I help other people because when I pray I realize that the "Christ in me" seeing the "Christ in them" makes me sensitive to their true needs. The contemplative monk and nun are probably more aware, even than the most diligent social welfare worker, of the cries of distress of our world. Their prayer life is their way in Christ of embracing all human suffering. Prayer is the contemplative's particular way of doing good. There is a contemplative side to me, and indeed to every Christian, which returns me time and again to the mystery of God and his will for our world. I take all the pain I encounter in my world and I give it to him. I can do no other or no better. In hospital wards, personal crises, homes filled with bereavement, God has chosen to rub off on to others through me only because I have allowed him entrance into my life. The Christian fellowship I give to another is the peace born of prayer, and, I repeat, the world is thirsting for it. It cannot abide by its counterfeit, and are we not guilty sometimes of that deception in our churches? The healing ministry is born out of our silent awareness of the needs of another.

It is not easy to learn the art of using periods of silence creatively. I hope I have grown spiritually in recent years because I have budgeted for these periods of silence in my life as the most precious moments of my day. When I look back over my earlier life I wonder how I survived without them. As a young priest I was preoccupied in "getting my prayers in", prayers which were just words and phrases bearing little or no relevance to my daily life. In some vague way they added to the noise in my life, and thus "prayers" were a sealed-off compartment of my spiritual bank into which I lodged my daily account. They were petrol for my spiritual car which was always on the go in a race against time. My prayers, however much I increased their quantity, did not make me a peace-filled person. Like many others in a similar situation I suppose I was afraid to listen to God lest in the silence he would slip through and call my bluff, and talk to me about the contradictions in my life style. I became so self-sufficient and self-righteous, in my "prayers" like the Pharisees, that soon I did not need God to talk to me. "Prayers" had become the substitute in which I foolishly believed I was talking to him.

My life did not change for the better, no matter what vast quantity of "prayers" I said, and it was only when I had to face real crises of faith in my life, like Jesus in the Garden, that I began to realize where I had gone so completely wrong. Jesus told us: "*In your prayers do not babble as the pagans do*, for they think that by using many words, they will make themselves heard" (Matthew 6:7). Prayer is not talking a great deal but loving a great deal. As they grow in love people do not feel the need for words as much as they did in their earlier years of courtship. What is true for individuals is also true for groups. What a tragedy it is that so many prayer groups are noisy, and when silence descends on the group someone feels compelled to start a hymn.

Just as in human relationships there is a time spent talking together about every conceivable subject, so there are times with God which I spend in silence. Although speech is a necessary means of communication, there is a whole world of spiritual exploration and discovery in which silence is the best and possibly only medium. There are many who believe that the best way to praise God is in words, whereas it is praise in the spirit within us that really counts. I know that we need vocal praise as well, but in this chapter I am trying to redress the balance of our noisy world and Church. Silence challenges me, and always will, because it opens up my life to God's voice and will for me in the world. It plunges me, as Thomas Merton says, "deep into the heart of the world in order to listen more intently to the deepest and most neglected voices that proceed from its inner depths." Silence with God does more for me than any words could. He brings me his peace in so far as I allow him to take over my life. "Be still and know" is no longer a phrase. It is a command, a challenge and a promise.

9

Not Being Disturbed
By Death And Dying

Serenity

Guilt and fear are two of the strongest emotions which adversely affect our peace of mind. Fear can so cripple us as to bring life to a standstill. In my experience the greatest fear surrounds death. How will we in fact die? Will it be painful? Will we die alone? And what of life after death? Can we really be so sure in our faith that there *is* a life after death? What part should the thought of death play in our normal pattern of thinking? The thought of death disturbs our peace, and yet I know that whether I like it or not I must die. My increasing bodily fatigue reminds me that I am on a downward slope. I am no longer able to do the same energetic things as in my youth. Even if I had a face-lift to cover up the wrinkles, I know that however much I may deceive others, I cannot escape the fact that I am getting older and that my inevitable death cannot be all that far away. And yet paradoxically there is no age for dying because death will come when it pleases, with no respect for age or persons. Dryden reminds us: "All human things are subject to decay, and, when fate summons, monarchs must obey." The young baby just delivered from its mother's womb is no more certain of life than an old man fighting, with his last reserves of energy, some dread disease. I am more certain that I shall die than that I shall see tomorrow; the baby dies, the old man limps on his troubled way, and death once more claims that it alone decides whom it takes to itself and when. This is why many people see death as cruel and disturbing of their peace. Through my Christian faith I have come to terms with it a long time ago, and it holds no fears for me.

Why is there this fear? The reason is that there is a finality about death which has a subduing influence on those who witness it. People speak in hushed whispers and even those in the family circle, who for years lived apart in hostile silence, are drawn together in reconciliation. They eulogise all the good things, real or imaginary, done by "the departed" as if they were afraid that he would come back to haunt them. Some of the funniest Irish stories concern "wakes" and funerals, which they use as a safety valve for their fear of death. People draw closer together in the presence of death not because of love but because of its opposite – fear. They huddle together, as if by their very closeness they hope to ward off death striking again. The very mention of death disturbs their peace.

Why do so many otherwise good Christians have this pagan attitude to death? Why does this obsessive fear of death persist even though we know we must all die? The answer is that we do not truly believe that death is but the beginning of our full life with the Risen Lord. "Christians", writes Hugh Lavery, "are those who actually celebrate a death, and see it as a seed sown and not a lamp quenched." "We know", says St Paul, "that when the tent that we live in on earth is folded up, there is a house built by God for us, an everlasting home not made by human hands, in the heavens" (2 Corinthians 5:1). Our bodies are only the outer covering which we must shed if we are to become our full "Christian selves", much as a caterpillar sheds its skin in order to become a butterfly. But we are afraid of the "shedding" process even though we should welcome death as a friend: "Blessed be God for our sister the death of the body" was a favourite saying of St Francis of Assisi.

Somewhere along the line we have got our Christian attitude to death wrong. We may believe in the resurrection but it does not flow into our everyday thinking. Whereas birth is a cause for celebration, death seems to have become a dreadful necessity to be avoided by every possible means. Even those engaged in the ministry of healing talk of raising people from the dead! This is a failure to appreciate that dying is an integral part of life, as natural and predictable as being born. God alone gives us life to enter the world and takes it back from us at death in order to introduce us to a new form of existence. *Death, like life, is God's gift, and to be afraid to die is in some ways an offence against him.* We do not trust God with our future after death. It is as if we were saying, "I am clinging to the life I have because I am afraid that I won't get a better life in the future – if there is one." Fear of death makes people hang on inordinately to life however tawdry it may have become. The selfish person who has never learned to die a little is overpowered by the thought of his death. He is too "rich" in his worldly hold on life and not "poor" enough "in spirit" to trust in hope to a loving God who alone will provide for him in the next life. He values his own judgement rather than God's. I suppose it is the final clinging to our "selfish self" in this last battle of dying before the "Christian self" emerges as the complete victor.

Yet death is for me the ultimate liberator from all fear. Paradoxically it frees me from the great fear of itself, and when I look on death in this liberating light I shall see it for what it is, a stage in the journey of life. In the third century Tertullian wrote of death: "There is nothing dreadful in that which delivers us from all that is to be dreaded." Why is it then that parents shelter children from witnessing death and dying, thinking they are protecting them from harm? My first experience of seeing anyone dying was when I was six. We were all gathered round my grandmother's bed, and prayed as she breathed her last. My parents insisted that this should be so, and how right they were. When my grandmother died my mother said she had "gone home to God", and since then my attitude to death has been just that – a "going home". When death and dying become a taboo subject in the family and society then we create a fear and a disturbing of our peace that need not be there. I have been fortunate. I have been taught to look on dying, not as the ultimate disaster, but as something I shall encounter one day. Kahlil Gibran, one of my favourite spiritual writers, also looks on death as the liberator: "What is it to cease breathing but to free the breath from its restless tides, that it may rise and expand and seek God unencumbered? Only when you drink from the river of silence shall you indeed sing. And when you have reached the mountain top, then you shall begin to climb. And when the earth shall claim your limbs, then shall you truly dance."

Despite all this, I love life so much that I do not want to die, not just yet anyway. For those who believe that life here on earth is all they possess then physical death is the ultimate, and to want to die with such a philosophy is tantamount to suicide. Death for the Christian, even with his philosophy, can be very hard to face, and it would be foolhardy to pretend otherwise. There are times when I am tempted to avoid it and run away from its seemingly harsh reality. But if I have the Christian courage to deal with death when it comes into my life, for example, through the death of a friend or near relation, and see it for what it is then it will help me to grow as a Christian and deepen my inner peace and faith. I am not only diminished by the death of every single person but I grow through it. It helps me to prepare for my own death which is in reality my "final crisis", and crisis means "turning point". If I go on living life to the full, through little dyings to selfishness one day at a time, then I am making the "turning point" of my journey, my own death and dying, all that much easier. A holy monk when asked what he would do if he knew he were about to die replied with a thoughtful smile, "I would go on sweeping the floor." Thank God, and through my hope grounded in the resurrection of his Son, I would do the same.

When I die a little to my "selfish self" every day, then my death, when at last it comes, will, to that extent, have lost its sting and victory. My earthly life is like the grain of mustard seed which must die in order that I may grow and live a new life. Death, then, is a precondition of living, and when I die to my "selfish self" I shall in proportion live to my true "Christian self". Unless the seed of my earthly life die, then all I shall have left is the seed itself, which was meant to be sown and die in the soil of my life on earth. In a strange way, which I do not fully understand, though I grow in appreciation of it when I suffer as a baptized Christian, I am grafted on to the life and death of Jesus: "Always, wherever we may be, we carry with us in our body the death of Jesus, so that the life of Jesus, too, may always be seen in our body" (2 Corinthians 4:10). This Christian concept of life through death, of "finding through losing", is essentially connected with the Gospel of Jesus, who died that we might live. It is the paradox of the Christian life. Death which disturbs our superficial peaceful earthly existence helps us eventually to rest in peace.

Let me translate this axiom of Christian spirituality into practical language. Selfish people do not fully live, and therefore are afraid of death. If I am too selfish to die to my "selfish self" then eventually, when I have to die, I shall have nothing eternal to show in my life. Death then becomes the ultimate end or the great vacuum when self disintegrates. If, on the other hand, I learn creatively to deal with life at every moment, then death will lose its fears for me. I shall courageously venture out during life into the unknown territory of the Christian pilgrim. Through my commitment to God – May I call you Father?, to my neighbour – May I be your friend?, I shall gradually discover my true "Christian self" – Aren't you glad you're you? – and in the process transcend the emptiness of superficial living.

When I commit myself in love to God and my neighbour I can face my final end in peace and joy, knowing that at least I have tried as a Christian to live my life well. I shall then return to the source of life after my journey on earth without losing anything of value on the way. I shall have completed the circle of life through death in which death is ultimately lost and life for ever found.

The Christian life is for me a constant series of growth experiences, and when I understand the growth-producing qualities not only of living but of dying, then I can learn to "die" and "grow" at any point I choose. This "dying to my selfish self" is my growing up in the spiritual life so that eventually when physical death comes I am free truly to live. In this sense my death is a *healthy* event if I use it properly, seeing it as a necessary step forward in my full life. The closing of the door to my earthly life is the opening of the same door to eternity. Life is the opposite side of the coin to death. I shall receive my final opportunity for growth when I am at death's door, for which I hope I shall have prepared myself by a series of "little dyings" in my journey through life. Nothing will thus become us more in life than the manner of our leaving it. I have found from my experience as a priest that self-centred people so cling to their own selfish form of life that the act of dying is a very hard one. However physically painful the act of dying may be for the Christian, it is as nothing compared to the deep personal, spiritual (psychological) agony of someone who has lived his life for himself alone. He has not prepared for death by a series of "little dyings" and must endure the whole process at once, with very little depth of spirit to face the final challenge to grow.

Yet what of life after death? Does it exist, and if so where will it be, and what will it be like? Dryden put these fears, which can disturb our peace, in succinct verse:

> Death in itself is nothing; but we fear
> To be we know not what, we know not where.

People are afraid of death because we doubt whether there is anything beyond the grave. If there is no life after death then what is there to hope for? A people without hope is, of course, doomed to fear. The whole of the teaching of the Early Church is that our Christian hope is based on the resurrection of Jesus Christ. St Paul emphasized time and again that "the mystery is Christ among you, your hope of glory" (Colossians 1:27). "Take a firm grip on the hope that is held out to us. Here we have an anchor for our soul, as sure as it is firm, and reaching right through beyond the veil where Jesus has entered before us and on our behalf" (Hebrews 6: 18–20). We are people who live and die in hope, a hope that is based on the life, death and resurrection of Jesus Christ. If we fear death then how can we say we are a people of Christian hope?

People quite wrongly have guilt feelings concerning their doubts about life after death, whereas I believe that the very questioning itself helps us to a deeper penetration of the great mystery of our faith in the resurrection of Jesus, on which our life in this world and the next hinges. Even the Apostles themselves doubted the resurrection of

Jesus from the dead: "Lastly, he showed himself to the Eleven themselves while they were at table. He reproached them for their incredulity and obstinacy, because they had refused to believe those who had seen him after he had risen" (Mark 16:14). For the Apostles death was so final that when Jesus died they felt that this was the end of everything. Their complete surrender to the absoluteness of death is a crumb of comfort for us in our doubting. Their doubt seems to excuse our own. The most obvious case of doubt concerns Thomas, who has since been given the prefix "Doubting" (John 20: 24–29). I like to call him "believing" Thomas. St Gregory, commenting on the slow surrender of Thomas, sees it as a "great help to strengthening our faith because his act of faith is fuller and more explicit than any other confession of faith in the resurrection recorded in the Gospels." The unwillingness too of the Apostles to believe the reports of the empty tomb is only overcome when the risen Jesus stands in their midst.

Each one of us has to set the strength of our faith in the Risen Lord against the finality of physical death in order to determine which is stronger. It is the final encounter between faith and fear. Even when I believe in life after death some fear of death may still remain, but at least I shall know it for what it is. My faith in everlasting life will increase, and my fear of death decrease as my personal belief in the resurrection of Jesus grows. If I am an Easter person, and really believe in life everlasting, then I should thrill with joy since I would have conquered the fear of the ultimate, which is death. The world, in the face of such faith, would begin to hope again in the true value of life as we Christians live it. As it is we Christians are often a hunched-up congregation overburdened with sin and guilt who come to church every week in order to "hedge our bets".

Even though we believe in life after death the nagging doubt still remains. This doubt or fear has to be brought out into the open and challenged by faith. Those who doubt challenge my faith, and if few share their doubts with me then perhaps I have a clear indication that maybe they think that I too have little faith in life everlasting. Life after death is the most wonderful promise held out to Christians, and yet we' share our hopes with so relatively few. It is quite surprising how many good church-going people have reservations about life after death. Recently I met a missioner's wife who quite categorically stated that her dead husband "was no more". She believed that "he had his heaven on earth and when he died that was the end of him". She was devoid of Christian hope, and was no better than the Saduccees who did not believe in life after death. St Paul reminded the Sanhedrin at his trial in Jerusalem: "It is for our hope in the resurrection of the dead that I am on trial" (Acts 23:6).

Even though we may think that we firmly believe in life after death our peace of soul may be disturbed by the death of a loved one. This is quite a common phenomenon which, when the time comes, we will learn to grow through. A typical case which illustrates this point concerns an excellent Christian whose husband died tragically after nearly twenty years of very happily married life. She seemed lost for a long time afterwards, and no longer seemed to be "alive" because she had lost her peace of soul. The friends who were constant callers after his death no longer came to visit her as frequently as before, and she was left more or less to face her sorrows alone. She continued her church work with more vigour rather than less, probably in order to help her to forget herself and her sorrow. She began to draw in on herself, and felt her home was a prison with memories of her husband. Yet she was afraid to go out socially because everything was a painful reminder of him.

One day we were talking about life after death, and while she blindly professed her belief in the resurrection, I kept on asking her why she was so sure, and if so why was she so sad? Eventually she broke down and confessed that she wondered herself if her husband was still alive. We read and prayed together – 1 Corinthians, chapter 15 – and her tears which flowed were of joy rather than sorrow. "Now," she said, "I believe that Jack is alive and we will never be parted." She was a different person from that day onwards, when she truly believed that for her husband, as for all who die in Christ, *life is changed not taken away*.

I am not so much afraid of death as the manner of my dying, because basically I am afraid of suffering. I was told as a young man studying for the priesthood to picture myself in my last agony, far away from my friends and loved ones, an image that chilled my heart and disturbed my inner peace. I do not agree with this approach to spirituality which breeds fear, and the relics of it are still deeply ingrained in me and in many Catholic priests. It does not take into account that when my turn comes to die the Lord will be with me as I pass through the valley of darkness. What really disturbed my peace in my youth, however, was the death of my mother. Her death cast its shadow over the whole family a long time before it happened. At the impressionable age of fourteen, through wearying weeks and months, I watched her disintegrate physically and finally die. I hated to see her suffer, and yet I was aware that I was powerless to help her. For months I dreaded the tension which eventually would come when the moment of death arrived. The picture of it is still vivid in my memory, as indeed is the peace with which she left our world. I bless my father that he told me what was happening to her, and took me step by step along the way.

As a priest I have suffered with dying people because those closest to them refused to share with them the truth of their physical condition when it was kinder and necessary for them to do so. Everyone then proceeded to live a sham, so that an artificial atmosphere was created which is a positive harm to everyone, especially the dying. If only we were more sensitive to each other, then we would know what is required of us, and so share the last precious days with our loved ones at a depth that would enrich us all.

I had to tell my father and eldest sister, Mary, that they were dying, and I am convinced from my experience that they were helped by my honesty and support and that, therefore, it was right for me to do so. We talked about death in a creative way so that they were helped to die more easily. Our relationship was unique through a sharing not only of pain, but of our deep faith in the resurrection. Through the Christian manner of their dying they diminished my own fear of it. I certainly want to be told when I am dying since I believe it is my right, as well as a gift, which helps me to prepare for meeting with my Father, in whom I shall find my fullness of peace.

Death will always remain, of course, a test of faith of the bereaved, and for a time I found it hard to accept the deaths of my parents and sister at the particular time. Mourning does not bring back the dead to life on earth, and so in common with everyone else I had to learn to live with my loss, knowing that my grief would mellow as I picked up the pieces of my life again, and moved forward in my daily living.

It is wrong, as some Christian ministers have done, to minimize bereavement. The way I have heard some of them preach unfeelingly at funerals has made me wonder whether they have ever experienced the panic, the emotional tension, the periods of depression, the stark moments when death seems to haunt us with its apparent triumph because death for a time is uppermost in the lives of the bereaved. It is in such moments that, heartbreaking though it may be, people must go on believing in life after death, when every natural inclination opposes it, and when only the bereaved themselves know a pain in their hearts which can be experienced and not described. They may even be told to "snap out of it", but wounds of the heart take a long time to heal before a new peace in a new situation can be found.

There is no panacea for bereavement since each one is unique, with its own peculiar set of circumstances. Eventually our lives will settle back to a more even keel, and the life and death of our loved one will take on more realistic proportions. It is how we lived with them in life that will determine our attitude to them in death. It is not wrong to mourn the death of our loved ones, but St Paul reminds us: "Make sure you do not grieve about them, like the other people who have no hope" (Thessalonians 4:13). Weeping over the death of a loved one is not against our faith in the resurrection. At the death of Lazarus Jesus wept, and the Jews said, "See how much he loved him" (John 11:36). Tears are necessary to afford the bereaved a relief from tension, but tears should not overshadow the belief in the resurrection which is there as an anchor when they are cast about on a sea of emotions.

There are two choices for the bereaved: to live in grief and remorse, with an uncontrollable sense of guilt that they had not been as kind to the deceased as they should have been, or to face their feelings and work them through. Jesus, after he had wept, took over the leadership in order to help the bereaved Mary and Martha: "Take the stone away" (John 11:39). We have to get on with living despite our awareness that in the death of our loved one we have lost part of ourselves. In a sense it is true that we have to "leave the dead to bury their dead" (Matthew 8:22). This may sound cruel, but we cannot spend the rest of our lives in unproductive remorse; our loved ones would not have it that way.

The churches could do much more in assisting the bereaved to recover their peace of mind, and to use the occasion to help them deepen their faith in life after death. If churches placed Jesus more at the centre of their preaching, then his resurrection would be the focus of attention in our thoughts and prayers, rather than our own death. Perhaps as Roman Catholics we placed too great an emphasis on the importance of Christmas, and looked on Easter more as the end of Lent rather than the celebration of our own *personal* victory over death in the person of Jesus Christ. The reformed liturgy is helping to redress the balance, but we have a long way to go before our people will become filled with the power of their resurrection in Christ the Lord. From now onwards the person of Jesus, holding back the stone of the tomb letting in the light of his Father's love to dispel the darkness of death, should be the picture to keep before me in my journey through life. When I am buried in my tomb by men, then with the risen Jesus I pass through the open door on the other side to my heavenly home. *Jesus is my resurrection*. As a Christian I believe, like the Jews, in life after death, but more than that; I believe that my resurrection comes through the person of Jesus Christ because, like peace, it is his precious gift to me as his follower. He says to me, "I am the resurrection", and the life I share with him is in his risen body.

The church that does not highlight sufficiently the central role of Christ in our *personal* resurrection must obviously condemn its followers to an obsessive interest in, and fear of, death. The more we preach death, the less we preach life. How few sermons have we heard about heaven for which we are destined, while hell, which is not our home, is preached far too often? The preacher sometimes merely projects his own personal fears, and many people have got "hang-ups" on death, judgement and hell which not only seriously interfere with their spiritual lives but also cripple their attitude to life itself and destroy their peace of soul.

The message of St Paul and the Early Church is simple and triumphant: Jesus in his person has given every Christian new life through his death and resurrection. When I live in the light of this liberating truth then I shall grow in the personal love of Jesus throughout my life. I shall be so close to him when death comes that I shall see it as a dissolving in order to be with him fully and for ever. The only thing that will be disturbed will be the tent of my mortal body. Death will have been swallowed up in victory. Peace will reign for ever.

10

Allowing Yourself To Be Healed

Openness

No one likes to be told that he is ill whether physically, emotionally or spiritually. He is even less likely to admit it to himself or to others. Yet we are all damaged or diseased people, and if we want deep inner peace we must acknowledge our weakness and allow ourselves to be healed. We know that in physical terms we draw closer to death every day because, in a sense, from the moment of birth we begin the process of dying. Not one person of the human race has ever escaped the ultimate in physical disease which is death. Its seeds grow relentlessly within us until eventually they suffocate our tenuous hold on life. In similar ways we are damaged in our emotions, spirits and souls because we are the descendants of Adam: "Sin entered the world through one man, and through sin death, and thus death has spread through the whole human race because everyone has sinned" (Romans 5:12). But Christ is the new Adam who has restored life: "For the wages paid by sin is death; the present given by God is eternal life in Christ Jesus our Lord" (Romans 6:23). Christ has promised us the fullness of life not only for our bodies but also for our souls: "I have come that you may have life and have it to the full." Sin and death are no longer the ultimate destroyers of our souls and bodies. The promise of life without end is the source of my Christian peace, because no matter how afflicted I may be I still believe that Christ is my life-giver: "I am the living bread which has come down from heaven. Anyone who eats this bread will live for ever; and the bread that I shall give is my flesh for the life of the world" (John 6:51).

Christ is our *healer*. He is the Divine Physician for all those who believe in him: "It is not those who are well who need the doctor," he said, "but the sick. I have not come to call the virtuous but sinners to repentance" (Luke 5:31). I know from long personal experience how ill I am in every aspect of my life because I live with the effects of sin. Christ heals me constantly not only in my body but in my emotions, my memory, my will and in the depths of my soul. All Christians are in a very true sense not only called to be healed but to heal. Christ's ministry to the sick is carried out today in the world which is a vast hospital and he uses us as his helpers. We either heal or hurt our world. Christians cannot be neutral or pass by on the other side of their wounded neighbour. To be a Christian is to be a healer. The Christian Church is a healing community and nowhere have I seen it more effectively in action than in the Maranatha Community.

Healing is an essential gospel word. It is sad that so few Christians fully understand what Christian healing really means. The root cause is because they have not experienced the full gospel meaning of the word. The word "healing", unfortunately, has sinister overtones for which we in the churches must bear most of the blame. It is often confused with faith healing and superstition. Roman Catholics as a rule place healing in a mainly spiritual context, and therefore confine it exclusively to the sacraments, whose ministers are the clergy. Healing is therefore a hierarchical function and privilege. If there is any physical healing to be acknowledged then this, as a rule, is attributed to people who have died and are in the process of being declared "Saints" by Rome, or is confined to places of special pilgrimage such as Lourdes and Fatima. Healing in its wider connotations is taken out of the ordinary, everyday life of Roman Catholics. Many Protestants, on the other hand, are so wrapped up in physical healing that they tend to ignore its deeper spiritual significance. They constantly seek signs and miracles as confirmation of their Christian belief. Recently a friend of mine who was a well-known evangelist made it known that he was suffering from terminal cancer. Thousands prayed for his physical recovery, and used him as a test case. They were shattered by his death, mainly because they did not understand the true meaning of healing, or the mystery of God's plan in suffering.

It is right therefore that in today's diseased world the whole question of Christian healing should be raised. What exactly does Jesus mean by "healing"? Does it mean that he protects me from every form of spiritual, emotional and physical disorder and disease? If after prayers for my healing I still remain ill is this due to my own lack of faith in the power of Jesus to heal me? If I really believed would I be able to overcome every form of disease? What is the difference between "being cured" and "being healed"? If Jesus is our healer why is it that Christians seem to be no different from others when it comes to the fears and phobias surrounding death and disease?

We need to look again at God's plan as revealed for us in the Bible if we are to understand what is meant by Christian healing. In the beginning God made us in his own image and likeness (Genesis 1:26). He wants us to be perfect, to be whole and healthy, and our destiny is to share our life with him through Christ who "is the image of the unseen God and the first-born of all creation. . . . God wanted all perfection to be found in him" (1 Colossians 15:19). Christ was to be "the eldest of many brothers" (Romans 8:29). This destiny is God's free gift to us: "Jesus

Christ will cause everyone to reign in life who receives the free gift that he does not deserve, of being made righteous" (Romans 5:17). "Before the world was made," says St Paul, "God chose us in Christ to live through love in his presence his free gift to us in the Beloved" (Ephesians 1:4,6). The same theme of God's overwhelming generosity to us is to be found time and again in the Old and New Testaments: "What is man that you should keep him in mind," writes the psalmist, "mortal man that you care for him? You have made him little less than a God; with glory and honour you crowned him. How great is your name, O Lord our God, through all the earth" (Psalm 8). To deny God's love for us, a Father who will not cause a needless tear, is to contradict the Bible and to remove us from even the faintest glimmering of any understanding of what is meant by Christian healing.

Christ was intended by God to be the crowning point of his creation. He is the person through whom our capacity for union with God was to be realized so that through him we might be "enabled to be adopted as sons" (Galatians 4:4). This sending of his Son into our world was his invitation to us to share the lot of the Son, and to come to the Father through him. God's free gift and purpose was to give us the opportunity to become his sons animated with his spirit, and so in Christ we are "stamped with the seal of the Holy Spirit of the Promise, the pledge of our inheritance which brings freedom for those whom God has taken for his own" (Ephesians 1:13–14). It is to reawaken and restore this awareness of the life and love of the Blessed Trinity within us that all Christian healing is directed.

Why do we need to be healed if we have such a glorious destiny? The simple answer is that being human we are part of our sinful human race. Destined to be taken into God's life in Christ by the power of his Spirit we rejected God's invitation. Man made of his world a world of sin, and so humanity could only be described as a fallen race. We became unhealthy and sin entered every aspect of our lives. We were diseased, not at ease with God, our neighbour or within ourselves. God was not deflected from his original plan and still wants us to share our true destiny, and so he sent his Son into our world, but now he comes as a healer and reconciler who "did not cling to his equality with God but emptied himself to assume the condition of a slave and he was humbler yet even to accepting death on a cross" (Philippians 2:6–8). Though personally sinless, he lived out his divine Sonship as man under the sign of sin: "For our sake God made the sinless one into sin so that in him we might become the goodness of God" (2 Corinthians 5:21).

It was his Father's will that perfect Sonship should be manifested in perfect obedience. This involved Christ laying down his life in testimony of his love for us – "A man can have no greater love than to lay down his life for his friends" (John 15:13). – and his love as a member of the human race for his Father. God is revealed as a saving Father whose generous, unlimited love overcomes our sinfulness: "God loved the world so much that he gave his only son, so that everyone who believes in him may not be lost but may have eternal life" (John 3:16). In response to the Son's testimony to him as a member of the sinful human race with whom he identifies, God the Father gives his testimony to the Son: "God raised him high and gave him the name which is above all other names so that all beings in the heavens, on earth and in the underworld, should bend the knee at the name of Jesus and that every tongue should acclaim Jesus Christ as Lord to the glory of God the Father" (Philippians 2: 9-11). Christ the Suffering Servant is revealed as the Lord who died and rose again for our sakes. In him a new age of righteousness is inaugurated: "For anyone who is in Christ there is a new creation: the old creation has gone, and now the new one is here" (2 Corinthians 5:17).

Christ the King of Glory is the healer who by his wounds heals us so that we share with him in his risen life. "When we were baptized in Christ Jesus we went into the tomb with him and joined him in death, so that as Christ was raised from the dead by the Father's glory we too might live a new life" (Romans 6:4). *Our healing is a restoration of the life we would have had if man had not sinned.* Like Christ we too must live under the sign of sin, but through his Spirit our healing is within us. Every time we ask for healing we call on the love and the life of the Blessed Trinity to come to our assistance; to the Father who created us, to the Son who died and rose again for us and to the Holy Spirit who dwells within us. "Didn't you realize that you were God's temple and that the Spirit of God was living among you?" (1 Corinthians 3:16). When we are called to share in Christ's ministry of healing and lay hands on people to heal them we do so in the power of the Holy Spirit to claim the victory already won by the Son, so that through the healing the Sonship of Christ may be acknowledged and glory given to God the Father's abiding love which transcends our sinfulness. It is in no other name or by any other power that healing takes place. It is to the Father's glory and not our own. Healing, therefore, is God the Father's gift to us in the Spirit of the Risen Christ. It is his will to restore all mankind to full Sonship with him who created man in the beginning in his own image and likeness. We do this by believing and acknowledging Jesus as Lord: "To all who did accept him he gave power to become children of God" (John 1:12). The circle is complete and Christ is the linchpin which secures our relationship with God. God's will for mankind is achieved through Christ. He is the dialysis machine which purifies our blood of its deadly disease. His death and resurrection are our antidote to sin.

Healing, like prayer, is unique. It varies from person to

person. It is an experience rather than theory, and I can write about healing only within the ambit of my own experience. What I write or say will make little or no impact on those who have no similar experience to which they can relate. Others will read this chapter and know that what is written is authentic because it speaks to them of the healing power of Christ which they have experienced in their own lives. I know that the most important element in all healing is the fact that I acknowledge before God that I need to be healed. Without it there is no healing. For years I suffered from a deep hurt with which I could not come to terms. I talked it over endlessly with friends. I prayed for deliverance from the hurt, but it would not go away because in some vague way I was afraid of being healed, much as a cripple comes to depend on his wheelchair and does not want to lose it. Keeping my hurt was like a drug because I could not face the pain only with my own strength. One day when I was alone in my own study I realized it was holding me back from loving God. I wanted to be an eagle but I was only a budgie singing in my cage about my hurt. I dared then to love and let the hurt go. I surrendered it to Christ, and it was like a huge weight being lifted off my shoulders. Life has not been the same since.

If Christ wants, and is able, to heal us, why is it that as a general rule we are so reluctant to admit that we need healing? This is an element in our chemistry as mysterious as the problem of suffering itself. I know from my dealings with people who come to be ministered to in healing that the most difficult part of the healing process is to make them aware of the hurt which they automatically screen from Christ's healing power, and even their own consciousness. Like alcoholics the first step in healing is an acknowledgement of the precise area which needs to be healed.

To define this precise area requires total honesty before

God and the gift of discernment. Many people with whom I have prayed have, in the beginning, asked for something quite different from their real needs, until gradually they were led to open the source of their hurt to the healing balm of Christ's healing touch. We have to define before the Lord what we need, much as the blind man who, having approached the Lord, was still asked by Jesus to say what he wanted. Healing involves change, and we all attempt to remain the complete masters of our own destiny and the source of our own peace. We are apprehensive about the kind of life Jesus will demand of us once we allow the full light of the Gospel to shine on those parts of our lives which up to now we have kept in the shadows. It is not a pleasant thing to admit that, despite all our prayers and apparent righteousness, we are still self-righteous and part of a fallen people damaged by sin whose effects we carry deep down inside us. We are very much Jekyll and Hyde characters, who appreciate St Paul's predicament, "I fail to carry out the things I want to do, and I find myself doing the very things I hate" (Romans 7:15).

Healing is not a once-for-all event but a constant and continuing process as necessary for us as the air we breathe. There is no healing or conversion so complete that we can say, "We are saved," because "We must be content to hope that we shall be saved" (Romans 8:24); no healing is so incomplete that we can pessimistically say, "I have been healed but because I have fallen there is no hope of further healing for me." After our initial healing we need further help from God, much as a patient needs convalescence after a serious operation. The reason why so many people at evangelistic missions "declare themselves for Christ" and then fall away is because we are all like pieces of land won back from the desert of the world, whose sands greedily reclaim what was once its own. Keeping healthy is a lifetime occupation for the Christian.

We cannot become or remain healthy by our own power. Too often in my life I have relied on my own resources and been thoroughly disappointed with the result of my achievements, or the lack of them. The mistake has been that I have tried to heal myself, and this is one of the main causes of the lack of peace and growth in many Christians. It is the Spirit alone who turns our whole lives towards the Lordship of Christ, for "no one can say, 'Jesus is Lord' unless he is under the influence of the Holy Spirit" (1 Corinthians 12:3). It is this reorientation by the Spirit towards the Lordship of Christ that heals us. He is the advocate promised to the Apostles (John 16:7–15), and conferred on them (Matthew 28:16–20). We are no longer alone in our struggle with our illness, the "selfish self" within us which places itself at the centre of our world. Healing, while the work of Father, Son and Holy Spirit, is very much the inspiration of the Holy Spirit. He is the main initiator.

Let me explain. All Christian healing is based on two principles. Firstly, we need to believe in and look on God as a loving Father, who cares for us and wants us to be healthy. However, we cannot call him "Father" in a way which heals us unless we are moved by the Spirit which "makes us cry out 'Abba, Father!'" (Romans 8:15). Secondly, when we ask for healing in Christ's name, to give not only glory to the Father but also proclaim the Lordship of Christ, we do so under the inspiration of the Holy Spirit. Through him we acclaim Jesus as Lord not with our mouths alone but deep down in our souls. Our healing therefore is divine in origin, continuation and consummation because however much we may yearn for the love of God our Father and desire to acknowledge Jesus as Lord of our lives, nevertheless we require a fundamental change of mentality, a conversion, before we can allow the healing love of God our Father to flow into our lives. This change or conversion is the work of the Spirit. We must also be humble enough to receive healing, discerning enough to acknowledge the root cause of our disease, and willing enough to change the pattern of our lives. All these are gifts of the Spirit who puts the will and action into us. In all these ways our healing is the work of the Holy Spirit.

I cannot explain why some receive the Spirit while others do not. It is the Father's will. Why some receive healing and others do not is as mysterious as the gift of faith itself. This has often puzzled us in the Maranatha Community. All we can say is that they are God the Father's free gift to us in the Beloved. The Spirit is sent to us by the Father and the Son. One of the great paradoxes in Christian healing is that we "receive" from the Holy Spirit in order "to be able to receive", and all this is due to God the Father's love for us as manifested in his Son Jesus Christ. A slow reading of Romans chapter 8 will help us to understand God's great gifts to us once he chose glory as our destiny. The rediscovery of the work of the Holy Spirit in our world, Church and lives has been the great blessing of our age. The Spirit which moves us to heal in the Maranatha Community is at the same time the source of our own healing.

Through the Spirit we come to look on God in faith as a healing Father. It is his love that heals not ours, because Christian healing in all its forms touches the soul of the person who is healed. Just as the various forms of "disease" ultimately have their roots in sin, so when God our Father heals us, for example, from memories which hold us back from living the full Christian life, he liberates our souls so that we may praise and proclaim the Lordship of his Son. All healing, however physical it may be, is for a spiritual purpose. We cannot overstress this divine dimension in healing, because there is no Christian healing without faith in God's power to achieve that which is beyond the scope of human effort, for "Who can forgive sins but God alone?" (Luke 5:21). It is this faith that was demanded by Jesus of all those who came for healing. "Your faith", he told the healed, "has made you healthy" (Matthew 9:22).

Christian healing is not faith healing because that is nothing other than autosuggestion. The techniques of stillness, creative thinking, controlling the body and the senses, are merely preparatory to the real work of healing which, as Christians understand it, can be performed by God alone and those who minister in the name of his Son. The techniques of faith healing are not to be rejected out of hand but seen and used for what they are, much as hospital staff prepare the operating theatre and patient for the real skills of the doctor. Because Christian healing touches the soul of the patient then it is never a cure in the generally accepted sense of the term, because a cure goes no deeper than the body and its symptoms. God alone goes to the source and root cause of our malady which lies deep in the soul. He alone is our healer.

We are not only healed but also called by the Spirit to share in the ministry of Christ's healing to others. In common with many others in our Maranatha Community, I have been called to such a ministry. Before every healing session in which I participate I always encourage those who take part to deepen their faith in God the Father's willingness to heal, their hope in Christ as Lord of their lives who has already conquered sin, death and the world, and their love of the Holy Spirit who is the inspirer of all healing, wholeness and health. The triangle of faith, hope and love is the area in which Christian healing takes place. There is no healing without obedience to God our Father, and it is above all in prayer that we surrender ourselves in obedience to the Father's will, because no matter what the outcome of the healing will be to outward appearances it will always be health-giving so long as we remember that as God's children we are "his heirs and coheirs with Christ, sharing his sufferings so as to share his glory" (Romans 8:17). God the Father never fails us. It is our discernment of what needs to be healed which is wrong if our prayers do not seem to be answered. The gift of discernment is paramount in any Christian healing community.

One of the greatest healings we can receive is that of a truly Christian understanding of suffering and how to use it creatively. Too many people over-emphasizing physical healing miss out completely on this great Christian truth. We share Christ's glory: we also share his sufferings. Recently I was called, with other members of the Maranatha Community, to the bedside of a woman dying of cancer, by a very emotionally upset husband, who in his heart wanted her to be physically healed. We had a double healing instead, of a completely different nature. The wife was given the grace of peacefully and compassionately enduring and using all her sufferings until the day she went to the Lord, and the husband was completely resigned to letting her go in peace. Death is never the victor in God's healing power.

Too often we so concentrate on physical healing that we forget to listen to and discern what God is saying to us. For Christians death is only the gateway to life without end. Do we want to go on physically healing those we love until they never die? Do we not realize that the body, tired by years in our world, has to let the soul go to be free so that we can be with the Lord? Is it not a greater healing sometimes to let the person be with God so that we may deepen our belief in the resurrection?

God's love never fails us. Whenever the Spirit calls us to take part in the healing ministry we must never lose sight of the Christian belief that God is limitless in his love. "Since God did not spare his own Son, but gave him up to benefit us all, we may be certain, after such a gift, that he will not refuse anything he can give" (Romans 8:32). It is our duty to call on the Spirit so that we pray according to the

Father's will and with a spirit of discernment. This discernment is vital to any Christian healing. To try to heal without it is like a surgeon operating on a patient without really knowing the nature and extent of his disease.

What I have written in this chapter is not theory but the result of hundreds of experiences in my own life as a Christian. When I look back with hindsight I realize that nothing which I appreciate as significant in my life has happened by chance. It is all part of God the Father's plan for me. Time and again I have been healed, whether through the sacraments of the Church, through people or events. I have always been deeply aware of the healing power of the sacraments through which on countless occasions my Christian life has been renewed. I believe we are all given the Holy Spirit in baptism, even though it may take us years to realize his power working within us. The sacrament of penance (reconciliation) has constantly repaired my relationship with God and my neighbour. Above all, the sacrament of the eucharist has been the great sacramental healing force in my life and it is towards that and from it that all my Christian healing flows, whether in receiving it or in ministering it to others.

People, too, have healed me, often without being conscious of what they were doing. At the age of five I was so seriously ill from food poisoning that three doctors had given my parents no hope for my survival. A good nun in the hospital wrapped me in a blanket and took me and my parents along to the convent chapel, where she offered my life to the Lord and prayed I would live to do great things for him. Within twenty-four hours I was off the danger list. I have no doubt the Lord used that simple, devout nun to be a minister of his healing, even though she would not know what I write about today on the subject of healing. She told me she did it because she was sorry for my parents and just asked God to spare me. It was as simple and profound as that. She was Christ's healer and I am alive today because of her faith in the God who could heal where doctors had failed.

In later life events too have been for my healing. I was healed more, and grew more, as a Christian through my desire to work for peace in Northern Ireland than through anything else. At first sight it caused me the greatest upheaval, turning my life upside down, and yet through it I have been given many precious insights into the Christian life. Without it the Maranatha Community would never have been founded. This book on peace, of whatever value it may be, is the direct result of my involvement in working for a just Christian peace in Northern Ireland. I have learned that I have to stand up and be counted for those principles in which I believe. In the process I know what it is to put honour from God before honour from men. I have grappled with human fear in the face of violence, with my only assurance that I was doing what God wanted me to do, and that I could not be anywhere else, or do anything else, and live at peace with my conscience. It has not been easy and is not so now, but I am beginning to get a glimmer of Jesus' beatitude: "Blessed are the peacemakers, they shall be called the sons of God" (Matthew 5:9). I have no ambition for a more fulfilling role. In my life too, as I get older, there has been a growing dependence on God alone as my Father, whose love can free me from guilt. Irrational guilt seems to plague us as Roman Catholics and hold us back from the full and free service of God. This is something from which we need liberating.

I have no idea what the future holds for me but I entrust it to his loving care. Through healing I can live one day at a time because he is with me, healing me every step of my pilgrimage. I know I shall find myself in hostile lands with little or no human support, but even though I walk in "the valley of the shadow of death no evil will I fear", because he has been there before me and has crossed in safety to the other side. I have a long road to travel but when I am weak and weary he will refresh me. In seeking his peace he heals me and offers me his own.

11

Learning The Meaning Of Obedience

Surrender

Obedience is an essential word in the Christian Gospel. Obedience to his Father's will is at the centre of the life of Jesus and is the source of his peace. Without obedience Christian peace has no meaning. No one can claim to be Jesus' follower unless he tries to live out this obedience in his own life. Jesus gave peace a new dimension, and obedience a new meaning, when he showed that his peace lay in absolute obedience to God his Father; all other forms of obedience were for him conditioned and secondary. If they did not flow from obedience to his Father then they were counterfeit.

At first glance "obedience" seems a simple, straightforward word, much as "peace", "love", healing" and other essential gospel words, but it is only when we probe deeper into them in the full light of the Gospel, and let them come alive in our own lives, that we begin to understand their awesome, challenging implications for ourselves and our way of life. Gospel obedience will always disturb my ordered way of life and yet unless and until we obey God absolutely we will never experience gospel peace.

Like peace, obedience costs nothing less than everything. The quality of our Christian life and peace is measured by the sacrifices we are prepared to make in order to do the Father's will. Jesus was "obedient unto death" (Ephesians 2:8). This is the yardstick of our obedience. If I really love

God as my Father and want to do his will then I must be ready to surrender everything I hold dear if this be his will for me. Obedience means that I trust my life in faith to God my loving Father and he will *reward* me with his Son's peace. This is the pattern of God's dealing with his people right through Jewish history. He rewarded those who obeyed him, much as he rewarded Abraham who was prepared to sacrifice his only child, Isaac, at his command. "All the nations of the earth shall bless themselves by your descendants as a reward for your obedience" (Genesis 22:18).

The reward of Jesus' obedience is that he, "the first of many brothers", brings peace, wholeness and salvation to all who believe in his message, and like him are obedient to his Father's will. He is greater than Abraham whom we call "our father in faith", and if we want to understand the full meaning of Christian obedience then we need to meditate on and imitate his life style. Obedience is written large in his life. From his earliest days he lived under its sign, which was a cross. When he was only eight days old his mother, Mary, in obedience to the command given by God to Moses to "consecrate all the first born to me" (Exodus 13:1), redeemed him who was sinless with the offering of the poor, "a pair of turtledoves or two young pigeons" (Luke 2:25). She was told by Simeon, even in the very act of total humble obedience, that though the child "was destined for the fall and rise of many in Israel – a sword will pierce your own soul" (Luke 2: 34–35). At the tender age of twelve Jesus severed the umbilical cord of permanent infanthood when he stayed behind in the Temple of Jerusalem in order to be "busy with his Father's affairs" (Luke 2:49), even though Mary and Joseph had been worried about his whereabouts. I believe this episode was the inspiration of his command to the Jewish people, "You must call no one on earth your father since you have only one Father, and he is in heaven" (Matthew 23:9).

This insight of God's sole claim to his obedience as his Father was the source of his obedience to Mary and Joseph. He put the fourth commandment of the Mosaic law in context. "He then went down with them to Nazareth and lived under their authority. He increased in wisdom, in stature and in favour with God and men" (Luke 2:51–52). In eighteen hidden years he grew intellectually, physically and spiritually, and in the process deepened his insight into the Fatherhood of God. He was the obedient Son of the Father in his public mission of reconciliation. "My meat is to do the will of the one who sent me and to complete his work" (John 4:34), even though this work would result in his death. In his agony in the garden his prayer for deliverance was conditional, "Father, if you are willing, take this cup away from me. Nevertheless, let your will not mine be done", (Luke 22:42), and when there was no deliverance from death on the cross he said, "Father, into your hands I commit my spirit" (Luke 23:46). The Father, to whom in obedience he committed his whole human life from start to finish, anointed him in the Resurrection as the King of Glory. This was his *reward* for obedience and we will share in it if like him we too are obedient.

What lessons have I learned for my own life from Jesus' obedience in my search for inner peace? The main lesson is that no matter what happens God the Father must remain supreme and absolute in my life. If I want to be at deep peace within my soul, then in faith I must surrender my life and leave the future to him. Only in this way can I live one day at a time, which alone is the recipe for gospel living. It is not easy to keep God as absolute in my life and never will be, because in common with most people I too seek the security of belonging to a group or system. I am afraid of being "the odd person out", of standing up and being counted, and so I tend to conform. It is so easy "to do as we are told" and to accept systems unquestioningly, without worrying too much about whether what we do is right or wrong. Yet if I am to practise gospel obedience then Jesus deprives me of the luxury of losing myself in a system. The trouble about laws is that they can be kept, whereas even in civil laws (as Lord Denning, former Master of the Rolls, says) the object of all laws is that they should promote justice, and thus put into effect the mind of the legislator. God's laws are rooted in love and are meant for our wholeness. This is God the Father's mind for us. "You must be perfect," says Jesus, "just as your heavenly Father is perfect" (Matthew 5:48).

Because they misunderstood that God's laws are for our healing and wholeness the Pharisees caught the brunt of Jesus' criticism. He castigated them for their over-observance of the letter of the law, especially of the inessential details, while blinding themselves to the whole spirit of the law. "The Sabbath," he said, "was made for man, not man for the Sabbath." Life for the Pharisees was rigorous and loveless. It led them not to righteousness or wholeness, but to self-righteousness and the disease of prejudice. "Alas for you, scribes and Pharisees, you hypocrites! You who pay your tithe of mint and dill and cummin and have neglected the weightier matters of the law – justice, mercy, good faith! These you should have practised, without neglecting others. You blind guides! Straining out gnats and swallowing camels!" (Matthew 23:23–24). The tragedy with laws and systems is that they can be kept, and often indeed scrupulously by those whose mentality and vision are far removed from the whole ethos and purpose of the laws. Such people are high on laws and low on love.

They see the law as supreme, and magnify it out of all proportion because they look at it from their own vantage point. They reduce God to their size and so determine his will for others with a maximum of assurance and severity and a minimum of prayer and mercy. Law becomes a barrier between God and his people. It is a God-substitute which increases religious observances and dilutes faith. It is a violation of the First Commandment, "I am your God. You shall have no God except me" (Exodus 20:2–3).

The system and its laws are corrosive not only of our spirituality but also of our humanity, when they intrude on our full and free obedience to God our Father. If we are to remain Christians within any formal church institution then we must always remain open to the questions the Spirit asks us. If we fail to do this then we fail in our duty as Christians. Unquestioning obedience has never been the hallmark of the saints and those whom the Spirit used in history to fashion the thinking and growth of Christ's followers down through the ages. The Early Church knew what was essential at the Council of Jerusalem. It is the same message in our present atomic age, namely, the Fatherhood of God and the Lordship of Christ as proclaimed in his Church to the various succeeding ages and cultures.

Obedience to the Father, which dominated the life of Jesus, is quite obviously the essential vocation of the Christian Church and therefore of every Christian. This can only be achieved by the Church and by individual Christians if they remain open to the Spirit. It is the same Spirit alone which enables us to look on God as a loving Father, which in turn liberates our faith from purely religious observance. This action of the Spirit in our lives is a continuing purifying process, because both we and the institutions we cherish live in a damaged world where power corrupts so quickly and insidiously. The greatest gift we can give to any institution is to remain open to the promptings of the Spirit. He will lead us and our churches into the fullness of truth. "True worshippers", said Jesus, "will worship the Father in spirit and in truth: that is the kind of worshipper the Father wants. God is Spirit, and those who worship must worship in spirit and truth" (John 4:24). If we love the Church as it is expressed in our communities, then we will constantly pray that God will be glorified in them. Institutions are not ends in themselves. They exist to facilitate and encourage our commitment to God our Father.

Unquestioning obedience to any institution is wrong. We owe institutions our *loyalty*; to God alone we give our *obedience*. Sometimes, however, there is a clash between loyalty to our institutions and the obedience we know deep within our consciences we should be giving to God. This is only to be expected. If we lived in a perfect world and Church, then both the institution and ourselves would be motivated by undiluted love of God the Father. I have only to look inside myself to know that this is not so. In living out my Christian faith I have never found gospel obedience an easy virtue to practise. At times it has left me feeling puzzled and alone, and yet I know that it was in these very moments of crisis that I grew as a Christian. My desire for obedience took me into the heart of Jesus' surrender to his Father. I have never been deliberately disloyal to my Church, while at the same time I have never allowed it to interfere with my obedience to God. On the contrary, its positive teaching and example from my earliest days as a child in Ireland helped me in my understanding of the Christian faith. For many years I have set the loyalty I give to my Church within the context of my obedience to God, and I have found that they feed each other in a way which nourishes my Christian life. *Loyalty is productive only when it flows from obedience*. The tragedy is that so many otherwise good Christians are trapped in the spider's web of meaningless customs and attitudes in their institutions which hinder rather than help their Christian growth. In the Maranatha Community we are fed by each other's Christian heritages and remain loyal to the church institutions which have spiritually fed us over the years.

Whenever there is a controversy in our Church institutions then we should spend our time in prayer, asking for the guidance of the Holy Spirit instead of wasting our energy and dissipating our faith in useless polemics. After prayer, through the inspiration of the Holy Spirit we will see the questions which disturb us in a new light because "When the Spirit of truth comes he will lead you to complete truth" (John 16:13). Controversy and rejection never disturb my peace in the depth of my soul because in the midst of the storm on the lake the Lord is with me, even though he seems asleep. It has not always been so. There have been times when I have allowed myself to be thrown off course by controversy. I am learning the ways of peace in the school of obedience and it is never easy.

Jesus knew what peace was even during his agony on the Cross. Although obedience to his Father's will cost Jesus his life he insisted, "I lay it down of my own free will. No one takes it from me", and he laid it down in obedience because "this is the command I have been given by my Father" (John 10:18). He loved his Father and knew that "the Father loves me because I lay down my life" (John 10:17). He laid it down in *love* which allowed him total freedom in his act of surrender. For Jesus, love was the touchstone of genuine obedience. He did not see the love of slaves as authentic obedience. For him freedom and obedience are two sides of the same coin. He trusted God with his life, and he saw his obedient service of the Father as perfect freedom.

All genuine Christian obedience flows from loving surrender of ourselves to the Father, and yet because we live with the effects of sin, and the claims of our "selfish selves", it is difficult for us to remain completely free. Our motivation is mixed, and our natural inclination is to seek the approval of others in our "group". We are more afraid of freedom than of the slavery of convention because we are not brave enough to stand with total honesty of purpose and courage behind our beliefs. This attitude is alien to the Gospel, whose full message never penetrates our conscience because of its disturbing influence in our lives. We are afraid of being rejected by others, and so we scale down our vision of life to that perceived by others. We fail the gospel challenge to grow, and settle for second-best, giving what obedience we can under the circumstances, but knowing in our innermost being that there was so much more we could and should have done and said. This double-think is astonishingly common in the institutional Churches, and the lament of Cardinal Wolsey, that he "had not served his God as well as he had served his King", is more often the cause for repentance among us clergy than those outside the institutions would like to imagine is possible.

Obedience is for my growth as a Christian person. Because I am redeemed by Christ and sanctified by his Holy Spirit I have to make use of all my faculties, especially my intellect and will, in my total surrender in obedience to the Father. Whenever I act under the pressure of blind conformity then I am destroying those very faculties which God himself respected when he first created the human race. God allowed us the freedom to sin and I must use my freedom to obey. Yet how few times do I really look at my responses to the Church, world and people and assess their true gospel value in relation to my obedience to God my Father? Obedience is not an anti-intellectual device designed to reduce our human judgements and assessments to the periphery of our Christian faith, because our obedience can never be irresponsible or slavish. I surrender in faith to God our Father those truths I do not understand by human reason. This is especially true in the realm of suffering. Cardinal Newman, whose prayer we have made our own in the Maranatha community, gives us precious insights into our trust in God's love and care for us: "God knows what he is about. He may take away my friends; he may throw me among strangers. He may make me feel desolate, make my spirits sink, hide my future from me – still he knows what he is about!" In faith we trust our lack of understanding, our doubts, our limited vision to God: "Who could ever know the mind of the Lord? Who could be his counsellor?" (Isaiah 40:13). Surrender to God in faith which flows from love is completely different from blind conformity which has fear as its source.

As soon as I associate obedience with passiveness then I cease to live the Christian life, and yet this is so common among so many otherwise excellent people in our churches. They seem to act unthinkingly as if by force of habit, and seem afraid to question anything in their institutions. Jesus condemned many of his listeners as being men of little faith. I have constantly to be on my guard against systems, or people who want to do my thinking for me. Life in the short term would be so much easier, but such passivity would prevent my growth in the Christian faith and my awareness of God as a loving Father who is interested in the pattern of my life. The only obedience recognized as Christian by the Second Vatican Council was *"active obedience"*, by which Christians through their creative response are willing to use their gifts and talents for the mission of the Church. Obedience then is for mission not submission. Like poverty its value is that it sets us free to show our love and trust in God our Father, who will provide not only for our material needs but also give spiritual significance to our lives, which may in the eyes of the world seem meaningless. Like Jesus in the Temple we are resolved "to call no man but God our Father". Our obedience, like that of Jesus, is childlike not childish because the Good News is revealed to the simple: "Jesus exclaimed, I bless you, Father, Lord of heaven and earth for hiding these things from the learned

and the clever and revealing them to mere children"
(Matthew 11:25). Simplicity flows from the deep well of
faith, and faith in God sets us free to live in true creative
freedom according to his will for us.

The Pharisees were men of religion not of faith. They
were the unthinking zealots of the New Testament, who
made life complicated for themselves and everyone else.
They were not free to love God in "active obedience"
because they observed all the laws down to the minutest
details, and in the process lost their true sense of freedom
and the need to grow in faith. Their *religion* suffocated
their *faith*. Conscious of them I have become increasingly
aware of the dangers of religion superseding the role of
faith in my life. Much as I owe to my Church, and those
who helped me to respect and be loyal to it, there will
always remain in my faith something in addition to the
creed I profess. It is the same, or should be, with every
practising Christian. God remains absolute in our lives.
While it is hard to explain in truly exact terms the
difference between religion and faith, nevertheless faith in
its origin and end is God's gift to his people, whereas
religion is how they in turn clumsily and under the shadow
of sin express it in words, action and culture. Faith breathes
life into religion! Without it religion becomes a meaningless
ritual and set of rules. Too much religion ends in religious
mania. We can never have too much faith. There must be
sufficient faith, like salt, to influence religion but "if salt has
become insipid, how can you season it again? Have salt in
yourselves and be at peace with one another" (Mark 9:50).
Faith expresses itself in a movement, religion in organization. Both are needed in our world but the proportion of
the mixture must be right. A little more faith and a little less
religion might be a recipe for all institutional Churches to
follow!

Faith is God's gift to us. We have restricted truth to

truths and obedience to laws. Jesus said "I am the truth" (John 14:6), and yet we have reduced our knowledge of him to dead formulae which can in no way encapsulate his dynamic force in our lives. St Paul reminds us "the Gospel came to you not only as words but as power and the Holy Spirit and as utter conviction" (1 Thessalonians 1:4). The reason religion does not compel our assent is that it does not always bear the genuine stamp and seal of the Holy Spirit. It leaves our world cold and untouched when it imitates the secular. As Christians, instead of talking of possessing the truth we should rather be talking about being possessed by it.

As I become increasingly open to the work of the Holy Spirit in my life and world I become decreasingly certain of many inessential truths which in former years loomed large in my life and consciousness. I recognize them now as inessential and accretions to the Christian faith. In the past they gave me a false sense of security, but now I see them as divisive, inward-looking and crippling of my Christian growth. In the same way I have become increasingly involved in the principal mysteries of my faith which show Christ to be the reconciler and bridge-builder for all who believe in his name, and proclaim the power of his Spirit at work in their lives. These truths compel because they clinch the whole of my being in an affirmation: "Yes, I believe this to be true. Without it life is meaningless and I am prepared to die for it." I can do no more for my own Church and people than by living out these truths in my own life, because in doing so I become increasingly obedient to God the Father. The gift I can give my institution is that of a lively faith through which I am obedient to God the Father by the power of the Holy Spirit. This attitude may cause suspicion and witch-hunting among the more conventional Christians, but its disturbance is minor compared to the inner gospel peace I experience. Thomas à Kempis says it all for me: "Have a good conscience and thou shalt ever have gladness!"

My peace which comes from gospel obedience lies in being open to the Spirit and like Jesus "growing in wisdom and in favour with God and men" (Luke 2:52). I cannot tell you how to be obedient in your life. The truth that God is my Father and Jesus is my Lord are the two great gospel truths in my life which set me free to grow in the wisdom of faith. This is the essence of the Christian Gospel of liberation. "To the Jews who believed in him Jesus said: 'If you make my word your home you will indeed be my disciples, you will learn the truth and the truth will make you free'" (John 8:31–32). "Before faith came," says St Paul, "we were allowed no freedom by the Law. When Christ freed us he meant us to remain free. Stand firm, therefore, and do not submit again to the yoke of slavery" (Galatians 3:23, 5:1). The freedom to obey comes from the Spirit and "Christians are told by the Spirit to look to faith for those rewards that righteousness hopes for" (Galatians 5:5). In faith I trust my life to God the Father whose will I obey. Any lesser form of "obedience" flows from that.

I cannot have the luxury of being certain that I am doing his will. I can only hope that I am. This is sufficient for my peace because I live by faith. In common with other Christians I attempt to live out the implications of the full Gospel in my life. We are his new family and this is the source of our spiritual bond. "Jesus was still speaking to the crowds when his mother and his brothers appeared; they were standing outside and were anxious to have a word with him. But to the man who told him this Jesus replied: 'Who is my mother? Who are my brothers?' And stretching out his hands towards his disciples he said, 'Here are my mother and my brothers. Anyone who does the will of my Father in heaven, he is my brother and

sister and mother'" (Matthew 12: 46–50). I share Jesus'
family by uniting my obedience with his, and in the process
I am one with him in his peace.

EPILOGUE

The Maranatha Community

My search for inner peace continues. It will always be so because I am a Christian pilgrim. In my search I have been helped by many people who would be amazed if I were to tell them what passed over from their lives to mine. My understanding of the Gospel has grown especially through personally experiencing its living message in other Christians. In the past decade my spiritual growth has accelerated through involvement in the Peace Movement in Northern Ireland, and the Maranatha Community here in England. I have received from them both far more than I could ever dare to return in grateful service. Ireland is the country of my birth, and I yearn for peace and justice for both Protestant and Catholic communities in that troubled land. I have seen at first hand the evil effects of political, social, religious and cultural divisions, and I sincerely believe that there can be no lasting peace until Christians cross the barriers and see themselves as brothers and sisters united in a common cause. The misunderstandings I have endured in my own life, and in my search for peace in Northern Ireland, are nothing compared to what they suffer every day in their lives.

The forgiveness, courage, generosity and long-suffering of the Northern Ireland people helped me to discover new prophetic insights into the Gospel, and the Christian life. Through my work in Northern Ireland I reached a stage in my life where the Holy Spirit led me to look for others to help me in my pilgrimage of peace. At the same time as I was searching, the Holy Spirit was moving in the life of Dennis Wrigley, a Methodist whose roots go back to John Wesley. He published a Statement in 1976 entitled "Methodism and the Future Church", whose prophetic message and appeal for deep Christian renewal evoked a response right across all the church denominations. Large sections of that Statement perfectly echoed parts of my book *Why are you Afraid*.

We met to discuss where God was leading his people and decided to call a meeting in Manchester in November 1981 to which we invited anyone who felt moved as we were by the Spirit. The response was staggering. We were joined by Anglicans, Evangelists, Methodists, Roman Catholics, Congregationalists, Baptists, Quakers, Salvationists, Presbyterians and others. That day the Maranatha Community was born. The graces and healings that flowed from that meeting and have been with us since will soon be put on record so that God's glory may be manifested in our lives.

We all wanted the movement to belong to the Holy Spirit alone. It was his inspiration in the beginning and would remain under his guidance. Because we wanted to see where God was leading us, the name Maranatha (loosely translated "Come, Lord Jesus, Come", Revelation 22:20) emerged as the essential hallmark of the movement. Maranatha is a prayer and a statement of our belief that Jesus is Lord of our lives, transcending all cultural and denominational barriers. We have no officers, no official structure, no blue-print for the future. We are a movement, not an organization. What our community will become depends solely on the Holy Spirit. If it is to die or increase is of little consequence, for we are a Kingdom Community whose prophetic role for the service of the Church in the world is obvious to the thousands who have shared in it.

Because of our personal commitment to our own denominations our community is a scattered one, bringing the full Gospel message of Christ to our own individual situations. We hope in the process to benefit our local churches and communities, to which we all owe so much. We are enriched spiritually by the wealth of each other's traditions, and we are dedicated to Christian unity. Everything in our community is positive and growing because it is the work of the Spirit.

Without the Maranatha Community I would never have been healed of the deep hurts which scarred my Christian life. I learned to forgive because in our community I had seen the power of the Holy Spirit releasing others from the stranglehold of hurtful memories. In turn I have been called to bring the ministry of inner healing and peace to hundreds of people who come to share our meetings. I have grown through our members in my understanding of creative suffering and the power of compassion. The New Life for which I yearned is being fulfilled in the lives of Maranatha people through their single-mindedness and openness to the Holy Spirit. We live one day at a time because we know God will provide.

Silence is indispensable for those who truly wait on the Lord, and the atmosphere of prayer at our meetings is tangible. Is it any wonder that the expectancy of fulfilment and healing is never in vain? God always honours his people who honour him. But the two things which single Maranatha out as something special are the love we have for each other in the Lord, and the wonderful inner healings which take place at every meeting. We are in short a prophetic, healing, loving Christian community. Our community meets a spiritual need and the spirit of discernment is very much at work among us.

We are obedient to God our Father. He will show us the way. We trust him with our lives and service. What he has done in the past he will do again in our time and through us. The Maranatha prayer by John Henry Newman sums up the spirituality of our movement. It encapsulates the present stage I am at in my Christian pilgrimage of peace.

"God has created me to do him some definite service: he has committed some work to me which he has not committed to another. I have my mission – I may never know it in this life, but I shall be told it in the next. I am a link in a chain, a bond of connection between persons. He has not created me for naught. I shall do good; I shall do his work. I shall be an angel of peace, a preacher of truth in my own place while not intending it – if I do but keep his commandments. Therefore I will trust him. Whatever, wherever I am. I can never be thrown away. If I am in sickness, my sickness may serve him; in perplexity, my perplexity may serve him. He does nothing in vain. He knows what he is about. He may take away my friends, he may throw me among strangers. He may make me feel desolate, make my spirits sink, hide my future from me – still he knows what he is about.

Maranatha!

Fount Paperbacks

Fount is one of the leading paperback publishers of religious books and below are some of its recent titles.

- ☐ THE WAY OF THE CROSS Richard Holloway £1.95
- ☐ LIKE WIND ON THE GRASSES Rita Snowden £1.95
- ☐ AN INTRODUCTION TO MARITAL PROBLEMS Jack Dominian £2.50
- ☐ I AM WITH YOU John Woolley £2.95
- ☐ NOW AND FOR EVER Anne Townsend £1.95
- ☐ THE PERFECTION OF LOVE Tony Castle £2.95
- ☐ A PROPHETIC PEOPLE Clifford Hill £2.95
- ☐ THOMAS MORE Richard Marius £7.95
- ☐ WALKING IN THE LIGHT David Winter £1.95
- ☐ HALF WAY Jim Thompson £2.50
- ☐ THE HEART OF THE BIBLE George Appleton £4.95
- ☐ I BELIEVE Trevor Huddleston £1.75
- ☐ PRESENT CONCERNS C. S. Lewis £1.95
- ☐ PSALMS OF PRAISE Frances Hogan £2.50
- ☐ MOTHER TERESA: CONTEMPLATIVE IN THE HEART OF THE WORLD Angelo Devananda £2.50
- ☐ IN THE HURRICANE Adrian Hastings £2.50

All Fount paperbacks are available at your bookshop or newsagent, or they can be ordered by post from Fount Paperbacks, Cash Sales Department, G.P.O. Box 29, Douglas, Isle of Man. Please send purchase price plus 22p per book, maximum postage £3. Customers outside the UK send purchase price, plus 22p per book. Cheque, postal order or money order. No currency.

NAME (Block letters) _____

ADDRESS_____

_____

_____